THE COMMUNIST MANIFESTO

Also available in the same series:

THE COMMUNIST MANIFESTO
The Political Classic

KARL MARX
FRIEDRICH ENGELS

With an Introduction by
TOM BUTLER-BOWDON

CAPSTONE
A Wiley Brand

This edition first published 2021
Introduction copyright © Tom Butler-Bowdon 2021

This edition of *The Communist Manifesto* is based on the English edition of 1888, translated by Samuel Moore and edited by Friedrich Engels, which is in the public domain.

Registered office
John Wiley & Sons Ltd, The Atrium, Southern Gate, Chichester, West Sussex, PO19 8SQ, United Kingdom

For details of our global editorial offices, for customer services and for information about how to apply for permission to reuse the copyright material in this book please see our website at www.wiley.com.

A catalogue record for this book is available from the Library of Congress.

A catalogue record for this book is available from the British Library.

ISBN 9780857088765 (cloth)
ISBN 9780857088789 (epdf)
ISBN 9780857088772 (epub)

Cover design: Wiley

Set in 12/16pt, NewBaskervilleStd by SPi Global, Chennai, India.

C9780857088765_201023

CONTENTS

AN INTRODUCTION

By Tom Butler-Bowdon

To understand *The Communist Manifesto*, you must understand the year in which it was published.

The revolutions, or 'Spring of Nations' of 1848 saw uprisings across Europe. Populations rose up against the continent's suffocating, corrupt monarchies, and demanded greater freedoms and democracy, including more voting rights and freedom of the press. There was clamour for a shift from feudalism and empire to the modern nation-state or republic.

The movement was also about better conditions and rights for workers. Few demanded genuine economic equality, but the vast chasm between the rich and poor could no longer be tolerated.

The revolutions involved coalitions of reformers, the bourgeoisie, and workers' movements. But because they were rather unorganized and often spontaneous, and had no institutional support, they could not be sustained.

Most of the uprisings had fizzled out by early 1849.

There were some achievements: France transitioned from a constitutional monarchy to a Second Republic (although it was short-lived), the Danish monarchy ended, serfdom was abolished in Austria, and the Netherlands got democracy. But in many places there was renewed censorship and suppression. In Hungary, the uprising was brutally quashed. In Germany, the Prussian government in Berlin put out the flames of nationalism and freedom along with the Federation's 39 states.

As reactionary forces reasserted themselves, intellectuals and reformers were imprisoned or forced into exile. One of these political exiles was Karl Heinrich Marx.

YOUNG PHILOSOPHER

The brilliant 30-year-old had been editor of the *Rheinische Zeitung*, a left-wing newspaper in Cologne, in Germany's Rhineland. Its banning by the authorities had forced him to move to Paris, and then Brussels – where *The Communist Manifesto* was written. We need to go back a few years, though, to understand the context in which the *Manifesto* came into being.

In 1841, Marx was doing a year of compulsory military service for the Prussian Army. He also submitted his final thesis for his Doctor of Philosophy degree (on the difference between the Democritean and Epicurean philosophies of nature). Because the thesis argued for the supremacy of philosophy over theology, Marx's conservative professors at the University of Berlin didn't like it. He had to submit the thesis at another university.

Marx already had some notoriety for being a member of the Young Hegelians, a group of students who called for a society based on reason and freedom. Over time, the group had become radicalized, and was highly critical of the Prussian state. Members believed that the state was not, as the great philosopher G.W.F. Hegel and his followers had argued, 'the fulfilment of history'. Rather, under the new king, Frederick William IV, a further clampdown on political and religious liberties meant that progress and history were being thwarted.

Marx had broken away from the Young Hegelians when he became dissatisfied with Hegel's conception of the world as an idea. No, Marx thought, the world is *physical* and it is within our power to shape society, economics and politics. In 1845 (in his *Theses on Feuerbach*) Marx had written: 'The philosophers have only interpreted the world in various ways; the point however is to change it.' Marx also rejected the spiritual foundations of the Prussian state. In the modern world, he thought, the state should exist on the basis of reason alone. It should serve all its citizens, not just a thin layer of aristocrats at the top.

We now take such ideas for granted, but in 1840s Germany they could threaten your job or put you in jail. That did not deter Marx, even though he was engaged to be married (to Jenny von Westphalen, the daughter of a free-thinking aristocrat) and was expected to begin a career and have a family. He had the reputation of being fearless.

Karl Marx in his thirties, London

CRUSADING JOURNALIST

Marx had begun writing articles for the *Rheinische Zeitung*. He was highly critical of the regional Rhineland government, whose laws and policies (including suppression of a free press) privileged the upper classes over the rest of society. These writings represent Marx's shift from politics and philosophy to economic questions and practical socialism. With academia apparently closed off to him (being Jewish didn't help), he had needed to find other avenues for his ideas. Journalism seemed the best arena to fight injustice.

But the *Rheinische Zeitung* was barely afloat financially, and the owners sought a change of direction to increase subscribers. Marx was given editorial control, and the newspaper's articles became more strident. Reader numbers rose, and the newspaper became one of the most influential in Germany.

The government in Berlin had hoped that Marx's journalistic baby would die on its own. When the opposite happened, the Cabinet (with the King's approval) felt compelled to take action. The newspaper was banned.

This act turned *Rheinische Zeitung* into a cause célèbre for Germany's intellectuals. But thousands of average citizens also signed petitions. Marx became a public figure, and was depicted in a political cartoon as Prometheus tied to a printing press, with an eagle (representing the Prussian state) pecking out his liver.

PARIS AND BRUSSELS

Marx needed to continue agitating and writing without the threat of imprisonment, so he exiled himself to Paris. As Paris was a centre of socialist ideas, the move proved to be a blessing in disguise.

In the French capital he befriended the anarchists Mikhail Bakunin and Pierre-Joseph Proudhon. Proudhon had in 1840 published *What Is Property?*, which famously concludes that 'property is theft'. Proudhon called for the nationalization of land and workplaces to be put under the control of peasants and workers.

Marx also began the most important friendship of his life: with Friedrich Engels. The pair had met briefly before in Cologne, but in Paris the relationship deepened. Marx had read Engels' articles on the terrible conditions of industrial workers in England (where his father owned a textile factory in Manchester). Engels believed that a socialist revolution could only happen through workers taking over the means of production, i.e. factories. It was madness that the producers of goods gained virtually nothing, with all profits going to owners.

Marx and Engels got involved with the League of the Just, a secret society which aimed to overthrow governments. With Arnold Ruge, Marx worked on the publication of the *Deutsch–Französische Jahrbücher* (German–French Yearbooks), which aimed to carry on the ideas in the *Rheinische Zeitung*. In the end only one issue was printed, in February 1844, because it was hard to get copies distributed in Germany. Nevertheless, the journal caught the attention of the French government, and under pressure from Prussian authorities, Marx and Ruge were expelled from Paris.

Marx and his family now moved again, this time to Brussels. Liberal Belgium was then a haven for European progressives, and Marx and Engels joined the underground organization the Communist League. The League was a kind of successor to the League of the Just, and it enabled Marx to maintain contact with his radical friends in Germany.

A younger Engels (aged 20–25)

THE WRITING OF THE *MANIFESTO*

In a Communist League conference in London at the end of 1847, Marx and Engels were asked to write a manifesto for the organization.

Originally they planned to make it a longish catechism (a set of belief principles laid down as questions and answers), but Engels suggested to Marx (see Appendix A) that it be written in a prose narrative style with a bit of history thrown in to give it more impact.

Engels had earlier in the year written a *Communist Confession of Faith* involving 22 questions and answers (see Appendix B). He had also published his *Principles of Communism*, another catechism (Appendix C).

With these two documents, plus some writings of the Communist League, Marx had a good foundation to work from. He had been having a busy time in Brussels, giving lectures and attending to his young family (now with three children). With some prodding, he finally submitted *The Communist Manifesto* to the Communist League in early February 1848.

Despite Engels' input, in the end the dramatic tone and style of the *Manifesto* was very much Marx's own, and Engels – always happy to play second fiddle to a man he believed to be great – made sure that people knew it.

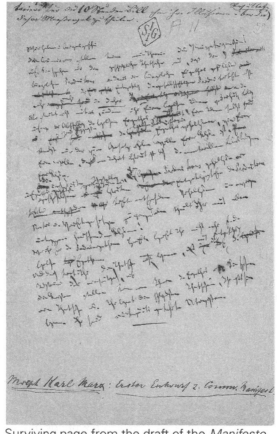

Surviving page from the draft of the *Manifesto*

PUBLICATION AND RECEPTION

Although first printed in London, the initial version of the text was in German, and did not credit Marx as author. Published as a pamphlet with the title *Manifest der kommunistischen Partei*, it was quickly serialized in the *Deutsche Londoner Zeitung*, a newspaper for German émigrés.

Reprintings soon followed. A thousand copies made their way to Paris, and the document circulated in Germany. Polish, Danish, and Swedish versions came out. The first English edition would not appear until 1850, when Helen Macfarlane's translation appeared in *The Red Republican*, a short-lived journal of the Chartist movement. Its editor, George Julian Harney, credited Marx as the author for the first time.

Was the *Manifesto* simply a reflection of the revolutionary *zeitgeist* of 1848, or did it have any actual impact on events?

Certainly not in France where, by the time it was published, revolutionary events were already in train. But as Germany broke out into semi-revolution, the *Manifesto* provided a rallying point. By this point Marx had moved back to Cologne, and had a new platform to speak from. He, Engels, and the Communist League had launched *Neue Rheinische Zeitung* at the start of 1848 to replace the old *Rheinische Zeitung*. It championed every kind of revolutionary movement in Europe and an overthrow of the continent's royal ruling houses, from the Habsburgs and Hohenzollerns to the Romanovs.

By May of 1849, the authorities had forced Marx's newspaper to close, and he was forced into exile again – this time to London. It was, again, arguably a blessing in disguise. In 1851, the Prussian police arrested members of the Communist League, and put them on trial in Cologne. The men were convicted, and sentences ranged from three to six years. But by this time, Marx, Jenny, and the children were safely ensconced in a flat in Dean Street in London's Soho. Marx would walk each day to the reading rooms of the British Library, where he was doing the research for the first volume of *Das Kapital*. He earned money by writing articles for the *New York Daily Tribune*. By 1856, the family had moved to a house in nicer Kentish Town, thanks to an inheritance Jenny received.

In 1872, Marx and Engels published a new German edition of the *Manifesto*, with a preface reflecting on the events of the Paris Commune of 1871 (when common people ran the government for two months). Over the years, and after Marx's death in 1884, Engels would add more prefaces, including to Samuel Moore's English translation in 1888, which he also supplied with notes.

Thus, a document that had begun life as a publication of an obscure political sect had now become 'a historical document which we no longer had any right to alter', as Engels put it. It had taken on a life of its own, inspiring and converting the masses across Europe and the world.

Cover of first edition of the *Manifesto*, in German but printed in London

A DARWIN FOR POLITICS

What does the *Manifesto* actually say? In the English edition, Engels puts it in a nutshell:

> [The] whole history of mankind (since the dissolution of primitive tribal society, holding land in common ownership) has been a history of class struggles, contests between exploiting and exploited, ruling and oppressed classes ... a stage has been reached where the exploited and oppressed class – the proletariat – cannot attain its emancipation from the sway of the exploiting and ruling class – the bourgeoisie – without, at the same time, and once and for all, emancipating society at large from all exploitation, oppression, class distinction, and class struggles.

In other words, it was not possible for the working classes to free themselves of domination simply by political and economic 'reform'. The only way it could happen was via a total revolution that forever reversed not just actual economic conditions, but the whole ideological basis of the class system.

Marx's ideas, Engels says in a footnote to the English edition, 'would do for history what Darwin's theory has done for biology'. Let's go deeper into the ideas in the *Manifesto*.

RISE OF THE MIDDLE CLASS

Marx and Engels write that Europe's old feudal system, based on static class relations and inherited property, is becoming obsolete. Traditions and social relationships are being swept away by a single common denominator: money. Old gradations in class according to birth, religion, and political allegiance are being replaced by possession of the means to exploit others for commercial gain. The guild system of closed trades and craftsmen is being pushed aside by the new dynamics of manufacturing and the division of labour.

Who were the winners in these tectonic shifts? Not the landed aristocracy, or the working classes, but the bourgeoisie. All the new wealth generated by manufacturing meant that the bourgeoisie could afford to buy their freedom from the feudal nobility that once held them under their thumb. The opening up of new territories around the world via imperialism, and increasing world trade, benefited this class hugely. European society was now coalescing into two monolithic masses: the bourgeoisie (the urban middle and commercial class of burghers and traders) and the proletariat (the working classes). The modern state, Marx and Engels say, had become 'but a committee for managing the common affairs of the whole bourgeoisie'.

They also say that the rise of the bourgeoisie is characterized by 'everlasting uncertainty and agitation'. Why? Because the desire for profit led to a lust for higher productivity. Every person's worth was now based on their 'exchange value'. This was a massive change from the past and its settled relations of economy and society. Or as Marx and Engels famously put it, 'All that is solid melts into air, all that is holy is profaned.'

WORKING CLASSES SINK LOWER

To be clear, Marx and Engels did not hate the explosion of technology and production unleashed in their time by the bourgeoisie and their dynamic deployment of capital, from the railways to canalization to mass agriculture. They were in awe of it.

What bothered them was the way capitalism ensured all the gains went to the owners of production, and very little to the actual, physical producers. Low wages were part of a conspiracy to keep workers at subsistence level: if all their energies had to go into simply putting bread on the table, they would not be thinking about political revolution.

In a communist system, the labourer's output would go to improve the life *of* the labourer. Factories and farms would be owned in common, and all would gain equally. The bourgeoisie protested that such a system would be the end of the individual's freedom to buy, sell, trade, and own. Yet how could the bourgeoisie be so shocked at the idea that property could be abolished, Marx and Engels ask, when nine-tenths of society were already held back from owning anything? Wasn't the extreme concentration of wealth, based on the exploitation of the many by the few, not the biggest injustice?

The worker had no say over how capital was deployed. His life and livelihood were 'exposed to all the vicissitudes of competition, to all the fluctuations of the market', exposed to cycles of boom and bust. Moreover, as the worker's job security falls, he also gives up the pride in work of the individual craftsman. He's just a cog in a monotonous factory machine. And since he is eminently replaceable, his wages go down. The factory owner, being in stiff competition with other capitalists, is naturally concerned to drive down prices (and wages).

Meanwhile, the small manufacturers, artisans, and shopkeepers that are still left are in time absorbed into an amorphous, larger proletariat. Their tiny resources cannot compete with the capital and organization of the industrialists, and their skills are made obsolete by new methods of production.

BOURGEOIS CONSPIRACY

Marx and Engels admit that a significant portion of the working classes, which they call the *lumpenproletariat*, are an unthinking mob who can become tools for reactionary and militaristic governments, such as the Prussian state or the Russian Tsar.

Yet all the time is emerging a more thinking, conscious proletariat that unites to try to raise class consciousness and force a rise in wages and better conditions, such as a shorter working day. Trade unions and political parties emerge which recognize that, in an economic system based on wage labour, the labourers actually hold the trump card.

Moreover, in a world in which all social relations are based on capital, it becomes obvious to the proletariat that things such as morality, culture, religion, and law are not 'universal' but rather bourgeois conspiracies to keep the worker and his family in their place. The fabled individuality and freedom of the bourgeois gentleman or lady rests on land rents and factory conditions that require worker exploitation.

The most shocking idea of the communists was the abolition of the family. What Marx and Engels mean is the abolition of the bourgeois family, who enjoyed the luxury of togetherness because they were not working all hours. Their nice house, possessions, and stability, not to the mention the means to become educated, sit on the back of the labourer, whose own children may be forced to work in a factory or go into prostitution. When it comes to the equality of women, Marx and Engels note that the bourgeois woman is a 'mere instrument of production' – just another thing to be exploited by the bourgeois male. Women under a communist system, on the other hand, would be liberated.

Marx and Engels here try to channel the brooding hatred of the bourgeoisie and upper classes felt by the legions of factory drones, below-stairs domestic workers, and tenant farmers. Without the ability to enjoy any property, this class feels as if it has nothing to lose and so becomes willing to overthrow the whole system.

THE ONLY WAY IS REVOLUTION

Marx and Engels note that, throughout history, the oppressed class was always given some means of elevation. During serfdom, for instance, the serf could raise himself up to become a member of a town commune, and therefore have some small power in relation to the nobility. But in the industrial age, the logic of capital and competition requires that more and more productive capacity must be squeezed out of the worker. He has little time or energy for social or community pursuits, and so his condition worsens as the wealth of the bourgeoisie increases. This fact provides the impetus for revolution, as workers in their fury unite.

The *Manifesto* excoriates the 'bourgeois socialists' who want to improve social conditions but are not willing to go through a revolution. This do-gooding bourgeoisie claims to work for society, but cannot or will not see that by seeking half-measures it is keeping the same system of class oppression in place.

Marx and Engels mention 'utopian socialists' such as Robert Owen in Britain, Charles Fourier in France, and Ferdinand Lassalle in Germany. America had its own socialist reformer in the form of Henry George. Then there was 'Christian socialism', which Marx and Engels see as a thinly disguised means for the upper classes to absolve their consciences concerning the plight of the working poor:

> The Socialistic bourgeois want all the advantages of modern social conditions without the struggles and dangers necessarily resulting therefrom. They desire the existing state of society, minus its revolutionary and disintegrating elements. They wish for a bourgeoisie without a proletariat.

Though some of these movements are well-meaning, in the end they are just attempts to reform the existing system without fundamental change in class relations. Marx and Engels respect Britain's Chartist movement, which they feel is quite close to the communists in outlook. But they do not think much of the German socialists of their time, who tinkered around the edges of society instead of committing to revolution. To succeed, you had to be unequivocal. Stirring words end the *Manifesto*:

> Let the ruling classes tremble at a Communistic revolution. The proletarians have nothing to lose but their chains. They have a world to win. Working men of all countries, unite!

AFTERMATH

By the late 1880s, Engel notes, the document had become 'the common programme of many millions of workers of all countries from Siberia to California'. Yet despite its notoriety and apparent rising support for communist ideas, Marxism hit a wall in the last decades of the nineteenth century.

Economies were doing well, and the prices of consumer goods were falling thanks to technology and productivity. Wages were rising and unemployment was low. Rather than becoming increasingly worse off under capitalism, as Marx had predicted, workers' lives were improving. As a result, workers' movements and trade unions were no longer (if they ever were) intent on overthrowing the capitalist order, but simply fought for better wages and conditions within it.

Indeed, after the crushing of dissent across Europe and the jailing of some socialists following the crises of 1848, Engels admits in his English preface that the *Manifesto* 'seemed doomed to oblivion'. Their big hope had been a revolution in Germany, which they believed was 'on the eve of a bourgeois revolution'. It had a more developed proletariat thanks to its advanced level of industry, but the imagined revolution never came. The International Working Men's Association had emerged as a force in Europe and America, but the 'struggle against capital' seemed infinitely hard and long.

Whereas the various strains of socialism have become almost acceptable to the middle class, communism remained a dangerous, worker-driven force whose success no country was prepared to countenance.

The fact is that the cogs of historical change moved much, much more slowly than Marx and Engels would have liked. Marx died in 1884 and Engels in 1895 – respectively three and two decades before the outbreak of the first Marxism-inspired communist revolution in Russia.

It now seems surprising that almost 70 years would pass between the publication of the *Manifesto* and the Russian Revolution of 1917. Ironically, Marx and Engels believed Russia would be one of the last places to fall to a workers revolution, such was the apparent power and influence of the Tsar, not only in Russia itself but across Europe. The Tsarist regime had intervened to crush the Hungarian revolution of 1848, and leaned on Prussia not to adopt a liberal constitution. At home, successive Tsars did their best to stop democratic reform, and urban workers grew to hate the excesses and aloofness of the royal family. In the countryside, most people were desperately poor. In such an environment, Mikhail Bakunin's 1882 Russia translation of the *Manifesto* had assumed the weight of scripture.

In other parts of Europe, democratic reforms had made revolution less likely. As the twentieth century began, a large split emerged between the die-hard theorists still bent on the overthrow of capitalism – including the German Communist Party of Karl Liebknecht and Rosa Luxemburg – and practical reformers best exemplified by the German Social Democratic Party, which simply sought better conditions for workers. In these years, *The Communist Manifesto* continued to represent the pole of revolution.

Soviet postage stamp commemorating the 100th anniversary of the *Manifesto*

CRITIQUE

What Marx and Engels did not foresee was the ability of liberal democracies to put capitalism *in the service of* the working class, instead of relentlessly exploiting it. The collectivization of the working class never happened in Western democracies because it was too large and varied to have a single political identity. Workers paid dues not to 'the working class' but to their particular union, which could effectively push for their interests within a specific industry.

Marx dismissed the willingness of workers to accept incremental improvements in conditions instead of revolution as mere 'economism', yet its power proved to be a flaw in Marxist philosophy. He did not foresee a time when workers would be given the opportunity to get an increasing share of capital indirectly through pension and savings schemes. A worker could own part of the company they worked for, or own a very tiny slice of many other companies. This shareholder economy would bring the interests of labour and capital closer together, if not into total alignment.

Marx and Engels decried the dangerous fluctuations of capitalistic markets, in which cycles periodically wiped out existing productive forces. But the flipside of this is what economist Joseph Schumpeter called 'creative destruction', a periodic clearing out of waste and unproductivity so that capital is deployed in the most efficient manner. Although individual businesses may fail, society as a whole moves forward.

In their distaste for conventional liberal economics, Marx and Engels were horrified by talk of prices and gain, seeing these as demeaning to human dignity because they turned the individual into a commodity. Greed and the profit motive were symptoms of a corrupt social system with the wrong priorities. Only by overturning the system itself would people be free. Yet this ignored the fact that buying and selling, and the price mechanism, had been proven for thousands of years as the best way humans had of working out the value of something. When you take it away, there is no longer any incentive on the part of the producer to produce something of higher worth or value, since no gain is to be made.

Marx also failed to see Adam Smith's basic logic that a society which allows everyone to pursue their selfish interests paradoxically can bring about a good allocation of resources overall. Perhaps against logic, such a society (rather than a planned one focused on equality) will quickly become richer, and not just those at the top. The old adage that capitalism succeeds because it has a low view of human nature, and communism fails because it conceives of humans too highly, is hard to refute.

Marx received frequent financial help from Engels, whose family owned a cotton mill in Manchester and had other business interests in Germany. Marx's mother Henrietta came from a wealthy Dutch Jewish family who would later start the Philips electronics company. Henrietta's brother, an industrialist and banker, helped out Karl and his wife Jenny with loans after they had settled in London. The family was able to move out of Soho to suburban Kentish Town thanks to an inheritance Jenny received from her upper-class father.

These facts indicated the extent to which money from capitalism enabled Marx to develop the theory of communism. Ironic, perhaps, but Marx saw his short-term financial difficulties as insignificant next to his role as the prophet of a new world.

Finally, there is a lack of detail in the *Manifesto*, and indeed in the later *Capital*, about how the economics of communism would actually work in practice. As Friedrich Hayek put it, 'If socialists knew anything about economics, they would not be socialists.' Once the aristocrats were gone and farms were operating with the new machines, how would it actually work? And where were the incentives to constantly innovate and make things better? Humans constantly need higher aims in order to live meaningful lives; just having enough to eat is not sufficient. That is perhaps the biggest criticism of communism: it misunderstood, or did not fully account for, human nature.

CONCLUSION

Even if communism as an economic system failed, it is not grounds for capitalist complacency.

As the French economist Thomas Piketty argues in *Capital in the Twenty-First Century*, advanced economies have in the last couple of decades shifted in emphasis from wage earning to capital owning. Wealth is increasingly concentrated, and social mobility has decreased. When the economic pie is growing bigger for all (as, for example, it did in most developed countries in the four decades following the Second World War) Marx seems irrelevant. But if the pie grows bigger for one group only, suddenly Marxist ideas about class and exploitation start to be meaningful again.

For capitalism to be humane, those who have worked to create the products or services that society needs must feel they are getting a proportionate gain. An unbalanced labour–capital equation may bring rebellion against 'the 1 per cent' and a rise of populist parties promising to throw out elites. Communism as a form of government may have manifestly failed, but this does not mean that Marx can be ridiculed. For if any system fails to properly give people a real chance to improve their lives, revolution will always be a real prospect.

For all its flaws, Marx's 'economic interpretation of history' showed how the economic environment and forms of production shape religion, art, philosophy, and institutions. One of Marx's achievements, said Joseph Schumpeter, is the reminder that 'it is our daily work which forms our minds, and that it is our location within the productive process which determines our outlook on things'. Whether owner, investor, or worker, our role and position within the productive process will be a major determinant of our happiness, and so warrants deep reflection.

Even if the system Marx and Engels envisaged was not fully practical, *The Communist Manifesto* is a timeless reminder to ask ourselves questions about fairness, and whether we are getting a just return for the hours and days we spend creating and producing.

Note on the Translation

This Capstone edition uses the 1888 translation by Samuel Moore, which was undertaken under Friedrich Engels' direction. The footnotes in this edition were added by Engels himself.

Through his work for the International Workingmen's Association, Moore had become the friend and sometimes legal adviser to Engels. Moore had translated the first volume of Marx's *Capital* (with Edward Aveling) in 1886, so he seemed a logical choice for taking on the *Manifesto*.

KARL MARX

Born one of nine siblings in 1818 in Trier in the Prussian Rhineland, Marx's grandfather and great-grandfather were rabbis, but his liberal lawyer father Heinrich converted the family to Lutheranism to avoid anti-Semitic laws preventing him from practising. Marx's mother Henrietta came from a wealthy Dutch Jewish family who would later start the Philips electronics company.

At Trier Gymnasium, Marx gained a solid grounding in Latin, Greek, French, and German. He attended university in Bonn and Berlin, then gained a doctorate from the University of Jena, but was considered too radical to be given an academic post. He married Jenny von Westphalen, of a Prussian aristocratic family, in 1843. They would have seven children.

In 1842, Marx began working for the radical *Rheinische Zeitung* in Cologne. After it was shut down by the authorities he moved to Paris, mixing with Pierre-Joseph Proudhon and anarchist Mikhail Bakunin, and becoming friends with Friedrich Engels.

Forced to leave Paris in 1845 after pressure from the Prussian state, he continued agitating from Brussels, penning *The Communist Manifesto*. After being thrown out of Belgium and refused entry to Germany, Marx moved to London in 1849. He was never granted citizenship, but lived there until his death in 1884.

FRIEDRICH ENGELS

Engels was born in 1820 in Barmen (now Wuppertal in Germany) into a Pietist family. He dropped out of school and was groomed to work in the family's cotton manufacturing business, but in his private time mixed with radicals.

His father hoped that a period working in the family's cotton mill in Manchester would moderate his views, but in 1845 he published in German *The Condition of the Working Class in England*, an exposé of the terrible factory conditions and child labour of the time.

From 1845 to 1848, Engels was with Marx in Brussels, and moved to London in 1849 to join him. His books include *The Peasant War in Germany* (1850), the anthropological *Origin of the Family, Private Property and the State* (1884), and *Socialism: Utopian and Scientific* (1880).

Engels believed marriage to be a bourgeois construct, but his partner of 20 years was the working-class Mary Burns. When she died in 1863, Engels formed a relationship with Mary's younger sister Lizzie. They were married just before her death in 1878.

After Marx died, Engels spent years editing the unfinished volumes of Marx's *Das Kapital*. Volume 2 was published in 1885, and Volume 3 in 1894. Engels died in 1895, his estate going to Marx's children.

ABOUT TOM BUTLER-BOWDON

Tom Butler-Bowdon is the author of the bestselling 50 Classics series, which brings the ideas of important books to a wider audience.

Titles include *50 Philosophy Classics*, *50 Psychology Classics*, *50 Politics Classics*, *50 Self-Help Classics*, and *50 Economics Classics*.

As series editor for the Capstone Classics series, Tom has written Introductions to Plato's *The Republic*, Machiavelli's *The Prince*, Adam Smith's *The Wealth of Nations*, Sun Tzu's *The Art of War*, Lao Tzu's *Tao Te Ching*, and Napoleon Hill's *Think and Grow Rich*.

Tom is a graduate of the London School of Economics and the University of Sydney.

www.Butler-Bowdon.com

THE COMMUNIST MANIFESTO

Karl Marx and Friedrich Engels

CONTENTS

PREFACE TO 1888 ENGLISH EDITION

The Manifesto was published as the platform of the Communist League, a working men's association, first exclusively German, later on international, and under the political conditions of the Continent before 1848, unavoidably a secret society. At a Congress of the League, held in November 1847, Marx and Engels were commissioned to prepare a complete theoretical and practical party programme. Drawn up in German, in January 1848, the manuscript was sent to the printer in London a few weeks before the French Revolution of February 24. A French translation was brought out in Paris shortly before the insurrection of June 1848. The first English translation, by Miss Helen Macfarlane, appeared in George Julian Harney's *Red Republican*, London, 1850. A Danish and a Polish edition had also been published.

The defeat of the Parisian insurrection of June 1848 – the first great battle between proletariat and bourgeoisie – drove again into the background, for a time, the social and political aspirations of the European working class. Thenceforth, the struggle for supremacy was, again, as it had been before the Revolution of February, solely between different sections of the propertied class; the working class was reduced to a fight for political elbow-room, and to the position of extreme wing of the middle-class Radicals. Wherever independent proletarian movements continued to show signs of life, they were ruthlessly hunted down. Thus the Prussian police hunted out the Central Board of the Communist League, then located in Cologne. The members were arrested and, after eighteen months' imprisonment, they were tried in October 1852. This celebrated "Cologne Communist Trial" lasted from

October 4 till November 12; seven of the prisoners were sentenced to terms of imprisonment in a fortress, varying from three to six years. Immediately after the sentence, the League was formally dissolved by the remaining members. As to the Manifesto, it seemed henceforth doomed to oblivion.

When the European workers had recovered sufficient strength for another attack on the ruling classes, the International Working Men's Association sprang up. But this association, formed with the express aim of welding into one body the whole militant proletariat of Europe and America, could not at once proclaim the principles laid down in the Manifesto. The International was bound to have a programme broad enough to be acceptable to the English trade unions, to the followers of Proudhon in France, Belgium, Italy, and Spain, and to the Lassalleans in Germany.*

Marx, who drew up this programme to the satisfaction of all parties, entirely trusted to the intellectual development of the working class, which was sure to result from combined action and mutual discussion. The very events and vicissitudes in the struggle against capital, the defeats even more than the victories, could not help bringing home to men's minds the insufficiency of their various favorite nostrums, and preparing the way for a more complete insight into the true conditions for working-class emancipation. And Marx was right. The International, on its breaking in 1874, left the workers quite different men from what it found them in 1864. Proudhonism in France, Lassalleanism in Germany, were dying out, and even the conservative English trade unions, though most of them had long since severed their connection with the International, were gradually advancing towards that point at which, last year at Swansea, their president [W. Bevan] could say in their name:

---

*Lassalle personally, to us, always acknowledged himself to be a disciple of Marx, and, as such, stood on the ground of the Manifesto. But in his first public agitation, 1862–1864, he did not go beyond demanding co-operative workshops supported by state credit.

"Continental socialism has lost its terror for us." In fact, the principles of the Manifesto had made considerable headway among the working men of all countries.

The Manifesto itself came thus to the front again. Since 1850, the German text had been reprinted several times in Switzerland, England, and America. In 1872, it was translated into English in New York, where the translation was published in *Woorhull and Claflin's Weekly*. From this English version, a French one was made in *Le Socialiste* of New York. Since then, at least two more English translations, more or less mutilated, have been brought out in America, and one of them has been reprinted in England. The first Russian translation, made by Bakunin, was published at Herzen's Kolokol office in Geneva, about 1863; a second one, by the heroic Vera Zasulich, also in Geneva, in 1882. A new Danish edition is to be found in *Socialdemokratisk Bibliothek*, Copenhagen, 1885; a fresh French translation in *Le Socialiste*, Paris, 1886. From this latter, a Spanish version was prepared and published in Madrid, 1886. The German reprints are not to be counted; there have been twelve altogether at the least. An Armenian translation, which was to be published in Constantinople some months ago, did not see the light, I am told, because the publisher was afraid of bringing out a book with the name of Marx on it, while the translator declined to call it his own production. Of further translations into other languages I have heard but had not seen. Thus the history of the Manifesto reflects the history of the modern working-class movement; at present, it is doubtless the most wide spread, the most international production of all socialist literature, the common platform acknowledged by millions of working men from Siberia to California.

Yet, when it was written, we could not have called it a *socialist* manifesto. By Socialists, in 1847, were understood, on the one hand the adherents of the various Utopian systems: Owenites in England, Fourierists in France, both of them already reduced to the position of mere sects, and gradually dying out; on the other hand, the most multifarious social quacks who, by all manner of tinkering, professed to redress, without any danger to capital and profit, all sorts of social grievances, in both cases men outside the working-class movement, and looking rather to the "educated" classes for support. Whatever portion of the working class had become convinced of the insufficiency of mere political revolutions, and had proclaimed the necessity of total social change, called itself Communist. It was a crude, rough-hewn, purely instinctive sort of communism; still, it touched the cardinal point and was powerful enough amongst the working class to produce the Utopian communism of Cabet in France, and of Weitling in Germany. Thus, in 1847, socialism was a middle-class movement, communism a working-class movement. Socialism was, on the Continent at least, "respectable"; communism was the very opposite. And as our notion, from the very beginning, was that "the emancipation of the workers must be the act of the working class itself," there could be no doubt as to which of the two names we must take. Moreover, we have, ever since, been far from repudiating it.

The Manifesto being our joint production, I consider myself bound to state that the fundamental proposition which forms the nucleus belongs to Marx. That proposition is: That in every historical epoch, the prevailing mode of economic production and exchange, and the social organization necessarily following from it, form the basis upon which it is built up, and from that which alone can be explained the political and intellectual history of that epoch; that consequently the whole history of mankind (since the dissolution of primitive tribal society, holding land in common ownership) has been a history of class struggles, contests between exploiting and exploited, ruling and oppressed classes; That the history of these class struggles forms a series of evolutions in which, nowadays, a stage has been reached where the exploited and oppressed class – the proletariat – cannot attain its emancipation from the sway of the exploiting and ruling class – the bourgeoisie – without, at the same time, and once and for all, emancipating society at large from all exploitation, oppression, class distinction, and class struggles.

This proposition, which, in my opinion, is destined to do for history what Darwin's theory has done for biology, we both of us, had been gradually approaching for some years before 1845. How far I had independently progressed towards it is best shown by my "Conditions of the Working Class in England." But when I again met Marx at Brussels, in spring 1845, he had it already worked out and put it before me in terms almost as clear as those in which I have stated it here.

From our joint preface to the German edition of 1872, I quote the following:

"However much that state of things may have altered during the last twenty-five years, the general principles laid down in the Manifesto are, on the whole, as correct today as ever. Here and there, some detail might be improved. The practical application of the principles will depend, as the Manifesto itself states, everywhere and at all times, on the historical conditions for the time being existing, and, for that reason, no special stress is laid on the revolutionary measures proposed at the end of Section II. That passage would, in many respects, be very differently worded today. In view of the gigantic strides of Modern Industry since 1848, and of the accompanying improved and extended organization of the working class, in view of the practical experience gained, first in the February Revolution, and then, still more, in the Paris Commune, where the proletariat for the first time held political power for two whole months, this programme has in some details been antiquated. One thing especially was proved by the Commune, viz., that "the working class cannot simply lay hold of ready-made state machinery, and wield it for its own purposes." (See The Civil War in France: Address of the General Council of the International Working Men's Association 1871, where this point is further developed.) Further, it is self-evident that the criticism of socialist literature is deficient in relation to the present time, because it comes down only to 1847; also that the remarks on the relation of the Communists to the various opposition parties (Section IV), although, in principle still correct, yet in practice are antiquated, because the political

9

situation has been entirely changed, and the progress of history has swept from off the Earth the greater portion of the political parties there enumerated.
But then, the Manifesto has become a historical document which we have no longer any right to alter."

The present translation is by Mr Samuel Moore, the translator of the greater portion of Marx's "Capital." We have revised it in common, and I have added a few notes explanatory of historical allusions.

Frederick Engels
January 30, 1888, London

MANIFESTO OF THE COMMUNIST PARTY

A spectre is haunting Europe – the spectre of communism. All the powers of old Europe have entered into a holy alliance to exorcise this spectre: Pope and Tsar, Metternich and Guizot, French Radicals and German police-spies.

Where is the party in opposition that has not been decried as communistic by its opponents in power? Where is the opposition that has not hurled back the branding reproach of communism, against the more advanced opposition parties, as well as against its reactionary adversaries?

Two things result from this fact:

I. Communism is already acknowledged by all European powers to be itself a power.
II. It is high time that Communists should openly, in the face of the whole world, publish their views, their aims, their tendencies, and meet this nursery tale of the Spectre of Communism with a manifesto of the party itself.

To this end, Communists of various nationalities have assembled in London and sketched the following manifesto, to be published in the English, French, German, Italian, Flemish and Danish languages.

I

BOURGEOIS AND PROLETARIANS*

---

*By bourgeoisie is meant the class of modern capitalists, owners of the means of social production and employers of wage labour. By proletariat, the class of modern wage labourers who, having no means of production of their own, are reduced to selling their labour power in order to live.

CHAPTER I

The history of all hitherto existing society[†] is the history of class struggles.

Freeman and slave, patrician and plebeian, lord and serf, guild-master[‡] and journeyman, in a word, oppressor and oppressed, stood in constant opposition to one another, carried on an uninterrupted, now hidden, now open fight, a fight that each time ended, either in a revolutionary reconstitution of society at large, or in the common ruin of the contending classes.

[†]That is, all written history. In 1847, the pre-history of society, the social organisation existing previous to recorded history, all but unknown. Since then, August von Haxthausen (1792–1866) discovered common ownership of land in Russia, Georg Ludwig von Maurer proved it to be the social foundation from which all Teutonic races started in history, and, by and by, village communities were found to be, or to have been, the primitive form of society everywhere from India to Ireland. The inner organisation of this primitive communistic society was laid bare, in its typical form, by Lewis Henry Morgan's (1818–1861) crowning discovery of the true nature of the gens and its relation to the tribe. With the dissolution of the primeval communities, society begins to be differentiated into separate and finally antagonistic classes. I have attempted to retrace this dissolution in The Origin of the Family, Private Property, and the State, second edition, Stuttgart, 1886.

[‡]Guild-master, that is, a full member of a guild, a master within, not a head of a guild.

In the earlier epochs of history, we find almost everywhere a complicated arrangement of society into various orders, a manifold gradation of social rank. In ancient Rome we have patricians, knights, plebeians, slaves; in the Middle Ages, feudal lords, vassals, guild-masters, journeymen, apprentices, serfs; in almost all of these classes, again, subordinate gradations.

The modern bourgeois society that has sprouted from the ruins of feudal society has not done away with class antagonisms. It has but established new classes, new conditions of oppression, new forms of struggle in place of the old ones.

Our epoch, the epoch of the bourgeoisie, possesses, however, this distinct feature: it has simplified class antagonisms. Society as a whole is more and more splitting up into two great hostile camps, into two great classes directly facing each other – Bourgeoisie and Proletariat.

From the serfs of the Middle Ages sprang the chartered burghers of the earliest towns. From these burgesses the first elements of the bourgeoisie were developed.

The discovery of America, the rounding of the Cape, opened up fresh ground for the rising bourgeoisie. The East-Indian and Chinese markets, the colonisation of America, trade with the colonies, the increase in the means of exchange and in commodities generally, gave to commerce, to navigation, to industry, an impulse never before known, and thereby, to the revolutionary element in the tottering feudal society, a rapid development.

The feudal system of industry, in which industrial production was monopolised by closed guilds, now no longer sufficed for the growing wants of the new markets. The manufacturing system took its place. The guild-masters were pushed on one side by the manufacturing middle class; division of labour between the different corporate guilds vanished in the face of division of labour in each single workshop.

Meantime the markets kept ever growing, the demand ever rising. Even manufacturer no longer sufficed. Thereupon, steam and machinery revolutionised industrial production. The place of manufacture was taken by the giant, Modern Industry; the place of the industrial middle class by industrial millionaires, the leaders of the whole industrial armies, the modern bourgeois.

Modern industry has established the world market, for which the discovery of America paved the way. This market has given an immense development to commerce, to navigation, to communication by land. This development has, in its turn, reacted on the extension of industry; and in proportion as industry, commerce, navigation, railways extended, in the same proportion the bourgeoisie developed, increased its capital, and pushed into the background every class handed down from the Middle Ages.

We see, therefore, how the modern bourgeoisie is itself the product of a long course of development, of a series of revolutions in the modes of production and of exchange.

Each step in the development of the bourgeoisie was accompanied by a corresponding political advance of that class. An oppressed class under the sway of the feudal nobility, an armed and self-governing association in the medieval commune[§]: here independent urban republic (as in Italy and Germany); there taxable "third estate" of the monarchy (as in France); afterwards, in the period of manufacturing proper, serving either the semi-feudal or the absolute monarchy as a counterpoise against the nobility,

---

[§]This was the name given their urban communities by the townsmen of Italy and France, after they had purchased or conquered their initial rights of self-government from their feudal lords. "Commune" was the name taken in France by the nascent towns even before they had conquered from their feudal lords and masters local self-government and political rights as the "Third Estate." Generally speaking, for the economical development of the bourgeoisie, England is here taken as the typical country, for its political development, France.

and, in fact, cornerstone of the great monarchies in general, the bourgeoisie has at last, since the establishment of Modern Industry and of the world market, conquered for itself, in the modern representative State, exclusive political sway. The executive of the modern state is but a committee for managing the common affairs of the whole bourgeoisie.

The bourgeoisie, historically, has played a most revolutionary part.

The bourgeoisie, wherever it has got the upper hand, has put an end to all feudal, patriarchal, idyllic relations. It has pitilessly torn asunder the motley feudal ties that bound man to his "natural superiors", and has left remaining no other nexus between man and man than naked self-interest, than callous "cash payment". It has drowned the most heavenly ecstasies of religious fervour, of chivalrous enthusiasm, of philistine sentimentalism, in the icy water of egotistical calculation. It has resolved personal worth into exchange value, and in place of the numberless indefeasible chartered freedoms, has set up that single, unconscionable freedom – Free Trade. In one word, for exploitation, veiled by religious and political illusions, it has substituted naked, shameless, direct, brutal exploitation.

The bourgeoisie has stripped of its halo every occupation hitherto honoured and looked up to with reverent awe. It has converted the physician, the lawyer, the priest, the poet, the man of science, into its paid wage labourers.

The bourgeoisie has torn away from the family its sentimental veil, and has reduced the family relation to a mere money relation.

The bourgeoisie has disclosed how it came to pass that the brutal display of vigour in the Middle Ages, which reactionaries so much admire, found its fitting complement in the most slothful indolence. It has been the first to show what man's activity can bring about. It has accomplished wonders far surpassing Egyptian pyramids, Roman aqueducts, and Gothic cathedrals; it has conducted expeditions that put in the shade all former Exoduses of nations and crusades.

The bourgeoisie cannot exist without constantly revolutionising the instruments of production, and thereby the relations of production, and with them the whole relations of society. Conservation of the old modes of production in unaltered form, was, on the contrary, the first condition of existence for all earlier industrial classes. Constant revolutionising of production, uninterrupted disturbance of all social conditions, everlasting uncertainty and agitation distinguish the bourgeois epoch from all earlier ones.

CHAPTER I

All fixed, fast-frozen relations, with their train of ancient and venerable prejudices and opinions, are swept away, all new-formed ones become antiquated before they can ossify. All that is solid melts into air, all that is holy is profaned, and man is at last compelled to face with sober senses his real conditions of life, and his relations with his kind.

The need of a constantly expanding market for its products chases the bourgeoisie over the entire surface of the globe. It must nestle everywhere, settle everywhere, establish connexions everywhere.

The bourgeoisie has through its exploitation of the world market given a cosmopolitan character to production and consumption in every country. To the great chagrin of Reactionists, it has drawn from under the feet of industry the national ground on which it stood. All old-established national industries have been destroyed or are daily being destroyed. They are dislodged by new industries, whose introduction becomes a life and death question for all civilised nations, by industries that no longer work up indigenous raw material, but raw material drawn from the remotest zones; industries whose products are consumed, not only at home, but in every quarter of the globe. In place of the old wants, satisfied by the production of the country, we find new wants, requiring for their satisfaction the products of distant lands and climes. In place of the old local and national seclusion and self-sufficiency, we have intercourse in every direction, universal inter-dependence of nations. And as in material, so also in intellectual production. The intellectual creations of individual nations become common property. National one-sidedness and narrow-mindedness become more and more impossible, and from the numerous national and local literatures, there arises a world literature.

The bourgeoisie, by the rapid improvement of all instruments of production, by the immensely facilitated means of communication, draws all, even the most barbarian, nations into civilisation. The cheap prices of commodities are the heavy artillery with which it batters down all Chinese walls, with which it forces the barbarians' intensely obstinate hatred of foreigners to capitulate. It compels all nations, on pain of extinction, to adopt the bourgeois mode of production; it compels them to introduce what it calls civilisation into their midst, i.e., to become bourgeois themselves. In one word, it creates a world after its own image.

The bourgeoisie has subjected the country to the rule of the towns. It has created enormous cities, has greatly increased the urban population as compared with the rural, and has thus rescued a considerable part of the population from the idiocy of rural life.

CHAPTER I

Just as it has made the country dependent on the towns, so it has made barbarian and semi-barbarian countries dependent on the civilised ones, nations of peasants on nations of bourgeois, the East on the West.

The bourgeoisie keeps more and more doing away with the scattered state of the population, of the means of production, and of property. It has agglomerated population, centralised the means of production, and has concentrated property in a few hands. The necessary consequence of this was political centralisation. Independent, or but loosely connected provinces, with separate interests, laws, governments, and systems of taxation, became lumped together into one nation, with one government, one code of laws, one national class-interest, one frontier, and one customs-tariff.

The bourgeoisie, during its rule of scarce one hundred years, has created more massive and more colossal productive forces than have all preceding generations together. Subjection of Nature's forces to man, machinery, application of chemistry to industry and agriculture, steam-navigation, railways, electric telegraphs, clearing of whole continents for cultivation, canalisation of rivers, whole populations conjured out of the ground – what earlier century had even a presentiment that such productive forces slumbered in the lap of social labour?

We see then: the means of production and of exchange, on whose foundation the bourgeoisie built itself up, were generated in feudal society. At a certain stage in the development of these means of production and of exchange, the conditions under which feudal society produced and exchanged, the feudal organisation of agriculture and manufacturing industry, in one word, the feudal relations of property became no longer compatible with the already developed productive forces; they became so many fetters. They had to be burst asunder; they were burst asunder.

Into their place stepped free competition, accompanied by a social and political constitution adapted in it, and the economic and political sway of the bourgeois class.

A similar movement is going on before our own eyes. Modern bourgeois society, with its relations of production, of exchange and of property, a society that has conjured up such gigantic means of production and of exchange, is like the sorcerer who is no longer able to control the powers of the nether world whom he has called up by his spells. For many a decade past the history of industry and commerce is but the history of the revolt of modern productive forces against modern conditions of production, against the property relations that are the conditions for the existence of the bourgeois and of its rule.

CHAPTER I

It is enough to mention the commercial crises that by their periodical return put the existence of the entire bourgeois society on its trial, each time more threateningly. In these crises, a great part not only of the existing products, but also of the previously created productive forces, are periodically destroyed. In these crises, there breaks out an epidemic that, in all earlier epochs, would have seemed an absurdity – the epidemic of over-production. Society suddenly finds itself put back into a state of momentary barbarism; it appears as if a famine, a universal war of devastation, had cut off the supply of every means of subsistence; industry and commerce seem to be destroyed; and why? Because there is too much civilisation, too much means of subsistence, too much industry, too much commerce. The productive forces at the disposal of society no longer tend to further the development of the conditions of bourgeois property; on the contrary, they have become too powerful for these conditions, by which they are fettered, and so soon as they overcome these fetters, they bring disorder into the whole of bourgeois society, endanger the existence of bourgeois property. The conditions of bourgeois society are too narrow to comprise the wealth created by them. And how does the bourgeoisie get over these crises? On the one hand by enforced destruction of a mass of productive forces; on the other, by the conquest of new markets, and by the more thorough exploitation of the old ones. That is to say, by paving the way for more extensive and more destructive crises, and by diminishing the means whereby crises are prevented.

The weapons with which the bourgeoisie felled feudalism to the ground are now turned against the bourgeoisie itself.

But not only has the bourgeoisie forged the weapons that bring death to itself; it has also called into existence the men who are to wield those weapons – the modern working class – the proletarians.

In proportion as the bourgeoisie, i.e., capital, is developed, in the same proportion is the proletariat, the modern working class, developed – a class of labourers, who live only so long as they find work, and who find work only so long as their labour increases capital. These labourers, who must sell themselves piecemeal, are a commodity, like every other article of commerce, and are consequently exposed to all the vicissitudes of competition, to all the fluctuations of the market.

Owing to the extensive use of machinery, and to the division of labour, the work of the proletarians has lost all individual character, and, consequently, all charm for the workman. He becomes an appendage of the machine, and it is only the most simple, most monotonous, and most easily acquired knack, that is required of him. Hence, the cost of production of a workman is restricted, almost entirely, to the means of subsistence that he requires for maintenance, and for the propagation of his race. But the price of a commodity, and therefore also of labour, is equal to its cost of production. In proportion, therefore, as the repulsiveness of the work increases, the wage decreases. Nay more, in proportion as the use of machinery and division of labour increases, in the same proportion the burden of toil also increases, whether by prolongation of the working hours, by the increase of the work exacted in a given time or by increased speed of machinery, etc.

Modern Industry has converted the little workshop of the patriarchal master into the great factory of the industrial capitalist. Masses of labourers, crowded into the factory, are organised like soldiers. As privates of the industrial army they are placed under the command of a perfect hierarchy of officers and sergeants. Not only are they slaves of the bourgeois class, and of the bourgeois State; they are daily and hourly enslaved by the machine, by the overlooker, and, above all, by the individual bourgeois manufacturer himself. The more openly this despotism proclaims gain to be its end and aim, the more petty, the more hateful and the more embittering it is.

The less the skill and exertion of strength implied in manual labour, in other words, the more modern industry becomes developed, the more is the labour of men superseded by that of women. Differences of age and sex have no longer any distinctive social validity for the working class. All are instruments of labour, more or less expensive to use, according to their age and sex.

No sooner is the exploitation of the labourer by the manufacturer, so far, at an end, that he receives his wages in cash, than he is set upon by the other portions of the bourgeoisie, the landlord, the shopkeeper, the pawnbroker, etc.

The lower strata of the middle class – the small tradespeople, shopkeepers, and retired tradesmen generally, the handicraftsmen and peasants – all these sink gradually into the proletariat, partly because their diminutive capital does not suffice for the scale on which Modern Industry is carried on, and is swamped in the competition with the large capitalists, partly because their specialised skill is rendered worthless by new methods of production. Thus the proletariat is recruited from all classes of the population.

The proletariat goes through various stages of development. With its birth begins its struggle with the bourgeoisie. At first the contest is carried on by individual labourers, then by the workpeople of a factory, then by the operative of one trade, in one locality, against the individual bourgeois who directly exploits them. They direct their attacks not against the bourgeois conditions of production, but against the instruments of production themselves; they destroy imported wares that compete with their labour, they smash to pieces machinery, they set factories ablaze, they seek to restore by force the vanished status of the workman of the Middle Ages.

At this stage, the labourers still form an incoherent mass scattered over the whole country, and broken up by their mutual competition. If anywhere they unite to form more compact bodies, this is not yet the consequence of their own active union, but of the union of the bourgeoisie, which class, in order to attain its own political ends, is compelled to set the whole proletariat in motion, and is moreover yet, for a time, able to do so. At this stage, therefore, the proletarians do not fight their enemies, but the enemies of their enemies, the remnants of absolute monarchy, the landowners, the non-industrial bourgeois, the petty bourgeois. Thus, the whole historical movement is concentrated in the hands of the bourgeoisie; every victory so obtained is a victory for the bourgeoisie.

But with the development of industry, the proletariat not only increases in number; it becomes concentrated in greater masses, its strength grows, and it feels that strength more. The various interests and conditions of life within the ranks of the proletariat are more and more equalised, in proportion as machinery obliterates all distinctions of labour, and nearly everywhere reduces wages to the same low level. The growing competition among the bourgeois, and the resulting commercial crises, make the wages of the workers ever more fluctuating. The increasing improvement of machinery, ever more rapidly developing, makes their livelihood more and more precarious; the collisions between individual workmen and individual bourgeois take more and more the character of collisions between two classes. Thereupon, the workers begin to form combinations (Trades' Unions) against the bourgeois; they club together in order to keep up the rate of wages; they found permanent associations in order to make provision beforehand for these occasional revolts. Here and there, the contest breaks out into riots.

Now and then the workers are victorious, but only for a time. The real fruit of their battles lies, not in the immediate result, but in the ever expanding union of the workers. This union is helped on by the improved means of communication that are created by modern industry, and that place the workers of different localities in contact with one another. It was just this contact that was needed to centralise the numerous local struggles, all of the same character, into one national struggle between classes. But every class struggle is a political struggle. And that union, to attain which the burghers of the Middle Ages, with their miserable highways, required centuries, the modern proletarian, thanks to railways, achieve in a few years.

This organisation of the proletarians into a class, and, consequently into a political party, is continually being upset again by the competition between the workers themselves. But it ever rises up again, stronger, firmer, mightier. It compels legislative recognition of particular interests of the workers, by taking advantage of the divisions among the bourgeoisie itself. Thus, the ten-hours' bill in England was carried.

Altogether collisions between the classes of the old society further, in many ways, the course of development of the proletariat. The bourgeoisie finds itself involved in a constant battle. At first with the aristocracy; later on, with those portions of the bourgeoisie itself, whose interests have become antagonistic to the progress of industry; at all time with the bourgeoisie of foreign countries. In all these battles, it sees itself compelled to appeal to the proletariat, to ask for help, and thus, to drag it into the political arena. The bourgeoisie itself, therefore, supplies the proletariat with its own elements of political and general education, in other words, it furnishes the proletariat with weapons for fighting the bourgeoisie.

Further, as we have already seen, entire sections of the ruling class are, by the advance of industry, precipitated into the proletariat, or are at least threatened in their conditions of existence. These also supply the proletariat with fresh elements of enlightenment and progress.

Finally, in times when the class struggle nears the decisive hour, the progress of dissolution going on within the ruling class, in fact within the whole range of old society, assumes such a violent, glaring character, that a small section of the ruling class cuts itself adrift, and joins the revolutionary class, the class that holds the future in its hands. Just as, therefore, at an earlier period, a section of the nobility went over to the bourgeoisie, so now a portion of the bourgeoisie goes over to the proletariat, and in particular, a portion of the bourgeois ideologists, who have raised themselves to the level of comprehending theoretically the historical movement as a whole.

Of all the classes that stand face to face with the bourgeoisie today, the proletariat alone is a really revolutionary class. The other classes decay and finally disappear in the face of Modern Industry; the proletariat is its special and essential product.

The lower middle class, the small manufacturer, the shopkeeper, the artisan, the peasant, all these fight against the bourgeoisie, to save from extinction their existence as fractions of the middle class. They are therefore not revolutionary, but conservative. Nay more, they are reactionary, for they try to roll back the wheel of history. If by chance, they are revolutionary, they are only so in view of their impending transfer into the proletariat; they thus defend not their present, but their future interests, they desert their own standpoint to place themselves at that of the proletariat.

The "dangerous class", [*lumpenproletariat*] the social scum, that passively rotting mass thrown off by the lowest layers of the old society, may, here and there, be swept into the movement by a proletarian revolution; its conditions of life, however, prepare it far more for the part of a bribed tool of reactionary intrigue.

In the condition of the proletariat, those of old society at large are already virtually swamped. The proletarian is without property; his relation to his wife and children has no longer anything in common with the bourgeois family relations; modern industry labour, modern subjection to capital, the same in England as in France, in America as in Germany, has stripped him of every trace of national character. Law, morality, religion, are to him so many bourgeois prejudices, behind which lurk in ambush just as many bourgeois interests.

All the preceding classes that got the upper hand sought to fortify their already acquired status by subjecting society at large to their conditions of appropriation. The proletarians cannot become masters of the productive forces of society, except by abolishing their own previous mode of appropriation, and thereby also every other previous mode of appropriation. They have nothing of their own to secure and to fortify; their mission is to destroy all previous securities for, and insurances of, individual property.

All previous historical movements were movements of minorities, or in the interest of minorities. The proletarian movement is the self-conscious, independent movement of the immense majority, in the interest of the immense majority. The proletariat, the lowest stratum of our present society, cannot stir, cannot raise itself up, without the whole superincumbent strata of official society being sprung into the air.

Though not in substance, yet in form, the struggle of the proletariat with the bourgeoisie is at first a national struggle. The proletariat of each country must, of course, first of all settle matters with its own bourgeoisie.

In depicting the most general phases of the development of the proletariat, we traced the more or less veiled civil war, raging within existing society, up to the point where that war breaks out into open revolution, and where the violent overthrow of the bourgeoisie lays the foundation for the sway of the proletariat.

Hitherto, every form of society has been based, as we have already seen, on the antagonism of oppressing and oppressed classes. But in order to oppress a class, certain conditions must be assured to it under which it can, at least, continue its slavish existence. The serf, in the period of serfdom, raised himself to membership in the commune, just as the petty bourgeois, under the yoke of the feudal absolutism, managed to develop into a bourgeois. The modern labourer, on the contrary, instead of rising with the process of industry, sinks deeper and deeper below the conditions of existence of his own class. He becomes a pauper, and pauperism develops more rapidly than population and wealth. And here it becomes evident, that the bourgeoisie is unfit any longer to be the ruling class in society, and to impose its conditions of existence upon society as an over-riding law. It is unfit to rule because it is incompetent to assure an existence to its slave within his slavery, because it cannot help letting him sink into such a state, that it has to feed him, instead of being fed by him. Society can no longer live under this bourgeoisie, in other words, its existence is no longer compatible with society.

The essential conditions for the existence and for the sway of the bourgeois class is the formation and augmentation of capital; the condition for capital is wage-labour. Wage-labour rests exclusively on competition between the labourers. The advance of industry, whose involuntary promoter is the bourgeoisie, replaces the isolation of the labourers, due to competition, by the revolutionary combination, due to association. The development of Modern Industry, therefore, cuts from under its feet the very foundation on which the bourgeoisie produces and appropriates products. What the bourgeoisie therefore produces, above all, are its own grave-diggers. Its fall and the victory of the proletariat are equally inevitable.

II

PROLETARIANS AND COMMUNISTS

CHAPTER II

In what relation do the Communists stand to the pro-letarians as a whole?

The Communists do not form a separate party opposed to the other working-class parties.

They have no interests separate and apart from those of the proletariat as a whole.

They do not set up any sectarian principles of their own, by which to shape and mould the proletarian movement.

The Communists are distinguished from the other working-class parties by this only: 1. In the national struggles of the proletarians of the different countries, they point out and bring to the front the common interests of the entire proletariat, independently of all nationality. 2. In the various stages of development which the struggle of the working class against the bourgeoisie has to pass through, they always and everywhere represent the interests of the movement as a whole.

The Communists, therefore, are on the one hand, practically, the most advanced and resolute section of the working-class parties of every country, that section which pushes forward all others; on the other hand, theoretically, they have over the great mass of the proletariat the advantage of clearly understanding the line of march, the conditions, and the ultimate general results of the proletarian movement.

The immediate aim of the Communists is the same as that of all other proletarian parties: formation of the proletariat into a class, overthrow of the bourgeois supremacy, conquest of political power by the proletariat.

The theoretical conclusions of the Communists are in no way based on ideas or principles that have been invented, or discovered, by this or that would-be universal reformer.

They merely express, in general terms, actual relations springing from an existing class struggle, from a historical movement going on under our very eyes. The abolition of existing property relations is not at all a distinctive feature of communism.

All property relations in the past have continually been subject to historical change consequent upon the change in historical conditions.

The French Revolution, for example, abolished feudal property in favour of bourgeois property.

The distinguishing feature of Communism is not the abolition of property generally, but the abolition of bourgeois property. But modern bourgeois private property is the final and most complete expression of the system of producing and appropriating products, that is based on class antagonisms, on the exploitation of the many by the few.

In this sense, the theory of the Communists may be summed up in the single sentence: Abolition of private property.

We Communists have been reproached with the desire of abolishing the right of personally acquiring property as the fruit of a man's own labour, which property is alleged to be the groundwork of all personal freedom, activity and independence.

Hard-won, self-acquired, self-earned property! Do you mean the property of petty artisan and of the small peasant, a form of property that preceded the bourgeois form? There is no need to abolish that; the development of industry has to a great extent already destroyed it, and is still destroying it daily.

Or do you mean the modern bourgeois private property?

But does wage-labour create any property for the labourer? Not a bit. It creates capital, *i.e.*, that kind of property which exploits wage-labour, and which cannot increase except upon condition of begetting a new supply of wage-labour for fresh exploitation. Property, in its present form, is based on the antagonism of capital and wage labour. Let us examine both sides of this antagonism.

To be a capitalist, is to have not only a purely personal, but a social *status* in production. Capital is a collective product, and only by the united action of many members, nay, in the last resort, only by the united action of all members of society, can it be set in motion.

Capital is therefore not only personal; it is a social power.

When, therefore, capital is converted into common property, into the property of all members of society, personal property is not thereby transformed into social property. It is only the social character of the property that is changed. It loses its class character.

Let us now take wage-labour.

The average price of wage-labour is the minimum wage, *i.e.*, that quantum of the means of subsistence which is absolutely requisite to keep the labourer in bare existence as a labourer. What, therefore, the wage-labourer appropriates by means of his labour, merely suffices to prolong and reproduce a bare existence. We by no means intend to abolish this personal appropriation of the products of labour, an appropriation that is made for the maintenance and reproduction of human life, and that leaves no surplus wherewith to command the labour of others. All that we want to do away with is the miserable character of this appropriation, under which the labourer lives merely to increase capital, and is allowed to live only in so far as the interest of the ruling class requires it.

In bourgeois society, living labour is but a means to increase accumulated labour. In Communist society, accumulated labour is but a means to widen, to enrich, to promote the existence of the labourer.

In bourgeois society, therefore, the past dominates the present; in Communist society, the present dominates the past. In bourgeois society capital is independent and has individuality, while the living person is dependent and has no individuality.

And the abolition of this state of things is called by the bourgeois, abolition of individuality and freedom! And rightly so. The abolition of bourgeois individuality, bourgeois independence, and bourgeois freedom is undoubtedly aimed at.

By freedom is meant, under the present bourgeois conditions of production, free trade, free selling and buying.

But if selling and buying disappears, free selling and buying disappears also. This talk about free selling and buying, and all the other "brave words" of our bourgeois about freedom in general, have a meaning, if any, only in contrast with restricted selling and buying, with the fettered traders of the Middle Ages, but have no meaning when opposed to the Communistic abolition of buying and selling, of the bourgeois conditions of production, and of the bourgeoisie itself.

You are horrified at our intending to do away with private property. But in your existing society, private property is already done away with for nine-tenths of the population; its existence for the few is solely due to its non-existence in the hands of those nine-tenths. You reproach us, therefore, with intending to do away with a form of property, the necessary condition for whose existence is the non-existence of any property for the immense majority of society.

In one word, you reproach us with intending to do away with your property. Precisely so; that is just what we intend.

From the moment when labour can no longer be converted into capital, money, or rent, into a social power capable of being monopolised, *i.e.*, from the moment when individual property can no longer be transformed into bourgeois property, into capital, from that moment, you say, individuality vanishes.

You must, therefore, confess that by "individual" you mean no other person than the bourgeois, than the middle-class owner of property. This person must, indeed, be swept out of the way, and made impossible.

Communism deprives no man of the power to appropriate the products of society; all that it does is to deprive him of the power to subjugate the labour of others by means of such appropriations.

It has been objected that upon the abolition of private property, all work will cease, and universal laziness will overtake us.

According to this, bourgeois society ought long ago to have gone to the dogs through sheer idleness; for those of its members who work, acquire nothing, and those who acquire anything do not work. The whole of this objection is but another expression of the tautology: that there can no longer be any wage-labour when there is no longer any capital.

All objections urged against the Communistic mode of producing and appropriating material products, have, in the same way, been urged against the Communistic mode of producing and appropriating intellectual products. Just as, to the bourgeois, the disappearance of class property is the disappearance of production itself, so the disappearance of class culture is to him identical with the disappearance of all culture.

That culture, the loss of which he laments, is, for the enormous majority, a mere training to act as a machine.

But don't wrangle with us so long as you apply, to our intended abolition of bourgeois property, the standard of your bourgeois notions of freedom, culture, law, &c. Your very ideas are but the outgrowth of the conditions of your bourgeois production and bourgeois property, just as your jurisprudence is but the will of your class made into a law for all, a will whose essential character and direction are determined by the economical conditions of existence of your class.

The selfish misconception that induces you to transform into eternal laws of nature and of reason, the social forms springing from your present mode of production and form of property – historical relations that rise and disappear in the progress of production – this misconception you share with every ruling class that has preceded you. What you see clearly in the case of ancient property, what you admit in the case of feudal property, you are of course forbidden to admit in the case of your own bourgeois form of property.

Abolition [*Aufhebung*] of the family! Even the most radical flare up at this infamous proposal of the Communists.

On what foundation is the present family, the bourgeois family, based? On capital, on private gain. In its completely developed form, this family exists only among the bourgeoisie. But this state of things finds its complement in the practical absence of the family among the proletarians, and in public prostitution.

The bourgeois family will vanish as a matter of course when its complement vanishes, and both will vanish with the vanishing of capital.

Do you charge us with wanting to stop the exploitation of children by their parents? To this crime we plead guilty.

But, you say, we destroy the most hallowed of relations, when we replace home education by social.

And your education! Is not that also social, and determined by the social conditions under which you educate, by the intervention direct or indirect, of society, by means of schools, &c.? The Communists have not invented the intervention of society in education; they do but seek to alter the character of that intervention, and to rescue education from the influence of the ruling class.

The bourgeois clap-trap about the family and education, about the hallowed co-relation of parents and child, becomes all the more disgusting, the more, by the action of Modern Industry, all the family ties among the proletarians are torn asunder, and their children transformed into simple articles of commerce and instruments of labour.

But you Communists would introduce community of women, screams the bourgeoisie in chorus.

The bourgeois sees his wife a mere instrument of production. He hears that the instruments of production are to be exploited in common, and, naturally, can come to no other conclusion that the lot of being common to all will likewise fall to the women.

He has not even a suspicion that the real point aimed at is to do away with the status of women as mere instruments of production.

For the rest, nothing is more ridiculous than the virtuous indignation of our bourgeois at the community of women which, they pretend, is to be openly and officially established by the Communists. The Communists have no need to introduce community of women; it has existed almost from time immemorial.

Our bourgeois, not content with having wives and daughters of their proletarians at their disposal, not to speak of common prostitutes, take the greatest pleasure in seducing each other's wives.

Bourgeois marriage is, in reality, a system of wives in common and thus, at the most, what the Communists might possibly be reproached with is that they desire to introduce, in substitution for a hypocritically concealed, an openly legalised community of women. For the rest, it is self-evident that the abolition of the present system of production must bring with it the abolition of the community of women springing from that system, *i.e.*, of prostitution both public and private.

The Communists are further reproached with desiring to abolish countries and nationality.

CHAPTER II

The working men have no country. We cannot take from them what they have not got. Since the proletariat must first of all acquire political supremacy, must rise to be the leading class of the nation, must constitute itself *the* nation, it is so far, itself national, though not in the bourgeois sense of the word.

National differences and antagonism between peoples are daily more and more vanishing, owing to the development of the bourgeoisie, to freedom of commerce, to the world market, to uniformity in the mode of production and in the conditions of life corresponding thereto.

The supremacy of the proletariat will cause them to vanish still faster. United action, of the leading civilised countries at least, is one of the first conditions for the emancipation of the proletariat.

In proportion as the exploitation of one individual by another will also be put an end to, the exploitation of one nation by another will also be put an end to. In proportion as the antagonism between classes within the nation vanishes, the hostility of one nation to another will come to an end.

The charges against Communism made from a religious, a philosophical and, generally, from an ideological standpoint, are not deserving of serious examination.

Does it require deep intuition to comprehend that man's ideas, views, and conception, in one word, man's consciousness, changes with every change in the conditions of his material existence, in his social relations and in his social life?

What else does the history of ideas prove, than that intellectual production changes its character in proportion as material production is changed? The ruling ideas of each age have ever been the ideas of its ruling class.

When people speak of the ideas that revolutionise society, they do but express that fact that within the old society the elements of a new one have been created, and that the dissolution of the old ideas keeps even pace with the dissolution of the old conditions of existence.

When the ancient world was in its last throes, the ancient religions were overcome by Christianity. When Christian ideas succumbed in the 18th century to rationalist ideas, feudal society fought its death battle with the then revolutionary bourgeoisie. The ideas of religious liberty and freedom of conscience merely gave expression to the sway of free competition within the domain of knowledge.

"Undoubtedly," it will be said, "religious, moral, philosophical, and juridical ideas have been modified in the course of historical development. But religion, morality, philosophy, political science, and law, constantly survived this change."

"There are, besides, eternal truths, such as Freedom, Justice, etc., that are common to all states of society. But Communism abolishes eternal truths, it abolishes all religion, and all morality, instead of constituting them on a new basis; it therefore acts in contradiction to all past historical experience."

What does this accusation reduce itself to? The history of all past society has consisted in the development of class antagonisms, antagonisms that assumed different forms at different epochs.

But whatever form they may have taken, one fact is common to all past ages, *viz.*, the exploitation of one part of society by the other. No wonder, then, that the social consciousness of past ages, despite all the multiplicity and variety it displays, moves within certain common forms, or general ideas, which cannot completely vanish except with the total disappearance of class antagonisms.

The Communist revolution is the most radical rupture with traditional property relations; no wonder that its development involved the most radical rupture with traditional ideas.

But let us have done with the bourgeois objections to Communism.

We have seen above, that the first step in the revolution by the working class is to raise the proletariat to the position of ruling class to win the battle of democracy.

The proletariat will use its political supremacy to wrest, by degree, all capital from the bourgeoisie, to centralise all instruments of production in the hands of the State, *i.e.*, of the proletariat organised as the ruling class; and to increase the total productive forces as rapidly as possible.

Of course, in the beginning, this cannot be effected except by means of despotic inroads on the rights of property, and on the conditions of bourgeois production; by means of measures, therefore, which appear economically insufficient and untenable, but which, in the course of the movement, outstrip themselves, necessitate further inroads upon the old social order, and are unavoidable as a means of entirely revolutionising the mode of production.

These measures will, of course, be different in different countries.

Nevertheless, in most advanced countries, the following will be pretty generally applicable.

1. Abolition of property in land and application of all rents of land to public purposes.

2. A heavy progressive or graduated income tax.
3. Abolition of all rights of inheritance.
4. Confiscation of the property of all emigrants and rebels.
5. Centralisation of credit in the hands of the state, by means of a national bank with State capital and an exclusive monopoly.
6. Centralisation of the means of communication and transport in the hands of the State.
7. Extension of factories and instruments of production owned by the State; the bringing into cultivation of waste-lands, and the improvement of the soil generally in accordance with a common plan.
8. Equal liability of all to work. Establishment of industrial armies, especially for agriculture.
9. Combination of agriculture with manufacturing industries; gradual abolition of all the distinction between town and country by a more equable distribution of the populace over the country.
10. Free education for all children in public schools. Abolition of children's factory labour in its present form. Combination of education with industrial production, &c, &c.

When, in the course of development, class distinctions have disappeared, and all production has been concentrated in the hands of a vast association of the whole nation, the public power will lose its political character. Political power, properly so called, is merely the organised power of one class for oppressing another. If the proletariat during its contest with the bourgeoisie is compelled, by the force of circumstances, to organise itself as a class, if, by means of a revolution, it makes itself the ruling class, and, as such, sweeps away by force the old conditions of production, then it will, along with these conditions, have swept away the conditions for the existence of class antagonisms and of classes generally, and will thereby have abolished its own supremacy as a class.

In place of the old bourgeois society, with its classes and class antagonisms, we shall have an association, in which the free development of each is the condition for the free development of all.

III

SOCIALIST AND COMMUNIST LITERATURE

CHAPTER III

1. Reactionary Socialism

A. Feudal Socialism

Owing to their historical position, it became the vocation of the aristocracies of France and England to write pamphlets against modern bourgeois society. In the French Revolution of July 1830, and in the English reform agitation* these aristocracies again succumbed to the hateful upstart. Thenceforth, a serious political struggle was altogether out of the question. A literary battle alone remained possible. But even in the domain of literature the old cries of the restoration period had become impossible.

In order to arouse sympathy, the aristocracy was obliged to lose sight, apparently, of its own interests, and to formulate their indictment against the bourgeoisie in the interest of the exploited working class alone. Thus, the aristocracy took their revenge by singing lampoons on their new masters and whispering in his ears sinister prophesies of coming catastrophe.

In this way arose feudal Socialism: half lamentation, half lampoon; half an echo of the past, half menace of the future; at times, by its bitter, witty and incisive criticism, striking the bourgeoisie to the very heart's core;

---

*Not the English Restoration (1660–1689), but the French Restoration (1814–1830).

but always ludicrous in its effect, through total incapacity to comprehend the march of modern history.

The aristocracy, in order to rally the people to them, waved the proletarian alms-bag in front for a banner. But the people, so often as it joined them, saw on their hindquarters the old feudal coats of arms, and deserted with loud and irreverent laughter.

One section of the French Legitimists and "Young England" exhibited this spectacle.

In pointing out that their mode of exploitation was different to that of the bourgeoisie, the feudalists forget that they exploited under circumstances and conditions that were quite different and that are now antiquated. In showing that, under their rule, the modern proletariat never existed, they forget that the modern bourgeoisie is the necessary offspring of their own form of society.

For the rest, so little do they conceal the reactionary character of their criticism that their chief accusation against the bourgeois amounts to this, that under the bourgeois *régime* a class is being developed which is destined to cut up root and branch the old order of society.

What they upbraid the bourgeoisie with is not so much that it creates a proletariat as that it creates a *revolutionary* proletariat.

CHAPTER III

In political practice, therefore, they join in all coercive measures against the working class; and in ordinary life, despite their high-falutin phrases, they stoop to pick up the golden apples dropped from the tree of industry, and to barter truth, love, and honour, for traffic in wool, beetroot-sugar, and potato spirits.[†]

As the parson has ever gone hand in hand with the landlord, so has Clerical Socialism with Feudal Socialism.

Nothing is easier than to give Christian asceticism a Socialist tinge. Has not Christianity declaimed against private property, against marriage, against the State? Has it not preached in the place of these, charity and poverty, celibacy and mortification of the flesh, monastic life and Mother Church? Christian Socialism is but the holy water with which the priest consecrates the heart-burnings of the aristocrat.

[†]This applies chiefly to Germany, where the landed aristocracy and squirearchy have large portions of their estates cultivated for their own account by stewards, and are, moreover, extensive beetroot-sugar manufacturers and distillers of potato spirits. The wealthier British aristocracy are, as yet, rather above that; but they, too, know how to make up for declining rents by lending their names to floaters or more or less shady joint-stock companies.

B. Petty-Bourgeois Socialism

The feudal aristocracy was not the only class that was ruined by the bourgeoisie, not the only class whose conditions of existence pined and perished in the atmosphere of modern bourgeois society. The medieval burgesses and the small peasant proprietors were the precursors of the modern bourgeoisie. In those countries which are but little developed, industrially and commercially, these two classes still vegetate side by side with the rising bourgeoisie.

In countries where modern civilisation has become fully developed, a new class of petty bourgeois has been formed, fluctuating between proletariat and bourgeoisie, and ever renewing itself as a supplementary part of bourgeois society. The individual members of this class, however, are being constantly hurled down into the proletariat by the action of competition, and, as modern industry develops, they even see the moment approaching when they will completely disappear as an independent section of modern society, to be replaced in manufactures, agriculture and commerce, by overlookers, bailiffs and shopmen.

In countries like France, where the peasants constitute far more than half of the population, it was natural that writers who sided with the proletariat against the bourgeoisie should use, in their criticism of the bourgeois *régime*, the standard of the peasant and petty bourgeois, and from the standpoint of these intermediate classes, should take up the cudgels for the working class. Thus arose petty-bourgeois Socialism. Sismondi was the head of this school, not only in France but also in England.

This school of Socialism dissected with great acuteness the contradictions in the conditions of modern production. It laid bare the hypocritical apologies of economists. It proved, incontrovertibly, the disastrous effects of machinery and division of labour; the concentration of capital and land in a few hands; overproduction and crises; it pointed out the inevitable ruin of the petty bourgeois and peasant, the misery of the proletariat, the anarchy in production, the crying inequalities in the distribution of wealth, the industrial war of extermination between nations, the dissolution of old moral bonds, of the old family relations, of the old nationalities.

In its positive aims, however, this form of Socialism aspires either to restoring the old means of production and of exchange, and with them the old property relations, and the old society, or to cramping the modern means of production and of exchange within the framework of the old property relations that have been, and were bound to be, exploded by those means. In either case, it is both reactionary and Utopian.

Its last words are: corporate guilds for manufacture; patriarchal relations in agriculture.

Ultimately, when stubborn historical facts had dispersed all intoxicating effects of self-deception, this form of Socialism ended in a miserable fit of the blues.

C. German or "True" Socialism

The Socialist and Communist literature of France, a literature that originated under the pressure of a bourgeoisie in power, and that was the expressions of the struggle against this power, was introduced into Germany at a time when the bourgeoisie, in that country, had just begun its contest with feudal absolutism.

German philosophers, would-be philosophers, and *beaux esprits* (men of letters), eagerly seized on this literature, only forgetting, that when these writings immigrated from France into Germany, French social conditions had not immigrated along with them. In contact with German social conditions, this French literature lost all its immediate practical significance and assumed a purely literary aspect. Thus, to the German philosophers of the Eighteenth Century, the demands of the first French Revolution were nothing more than the demands of "Practical Reason" in general, and the utterance of the will of the revolutionary French bourgeoisie signified, in their eyes, the laws of pure Will, of Will as it was bound to be, of true human Will generally.

The work of the German *literati* consisted solely in bringing the new French ideas into harmony with their ancient philosophical conscience, or rather, in annexing the French ideas without deserting their own philosophic point of view.

This annexation took place in the same way in which a foreign language is appropriated, namely, by translation.

It is well known how the monks wrote silly lives of Catholic Saints *over* the manuscripts on which the classical works of ancient heathendom had been written. The German *literati* reversed this process with the profane French literature. They wrote their philosophical nonsense beneath the French original. For instance, beneath the French criticism of the economic functions of money, they wrote "Alienation of Humanity", and beneath the French criticism of the bourgeois state they wrote "Dethronement of the Category of the General", and so forth.

The introduction of these philosophical phrases at the back of the French historical criticisms, they dubbed "Philosophy of Action", "True Socialism", "German Science of Socialism", "Philosophical Foundation of Socialism", and so on.

The French Socialist and Communist literature was thus completely emasculated. And, since it ceased in the hands of the German to express the struggle of one class with the other, he felt conscious of having overcome "French one-sidedness" and of representing, not true requirements, but the requirements of Truth; not the interests of the proletariat, but the interests of Human Nature, of Man in general, who belongs to no class, has no reality, who exists only in the misty realm of philosophical fantasy.

This German socialism, which took its schoolboy task so seriously and solemnly, and extolled its poor stock-in-trade in such a mountebank fashion, meanwhile gradually lost its pedantic innocence.

The fight of the Germans, and especially of the Prussian bourgeoisie, against feudal aristocracy and absolute monarchy, in other words, the liberal movement, became more earnest.

By this, the long-wished for opportunity was offered to "True" Socialism of confronting the political movement with the Socialist demands, of hurling the traditional anathemas against liberalism, against representative government, against bourgeois competition, bourgeois freedom of the press, bourgeois legislation, bourgeois liberty and equality, and of preaching to the masses that they had nothing to gain, and everything to lose, by this bourgeois movement. German Socialism forgot, in the nick of time, that the French criticism, whose silly echo it was, presupposed the existence of modern bourgeois society, with its corresponding economic conditions of existence, and the political constitution adapted thereto, the very things those attainment was the object of the pending struggle in Germany.

To the absolute governments, with their following of parsons, professors, country squires, and officials, it served as a welcome scarecrow against the threatening bourgeoisie.

It was a sweet finish, after the bitter pills of flogging and bullets, with which these same governments, just at that time, dosed the German working-class risings.

While this "True" Socialism thus served the government as a weapon for fighting the German bourgeoisie, it, at the same time, directly represented a reactionary interest, the interest of German Philistines. In Germany, the *petty-bourgeois* class, a relic of the sixteenth century, and since then constantly cropping up again under the various forms, is the real social basis of the existing state of things.

To preserve this class is to preserve the existing state of things in Germany. The industrial and political supremacy of the bourgeoisie threatens it with certain destruction – on the one hand, from the concentration of capital; on the other, from the rise of a revolutionary proletariat. "True" Socialism appeared to kill these two birds with one stone. It spread like an epidcmic.

The robe of speculative cobwebs, embroidered with flowers of rhetoric, steeped in the dew of sickly sentiment, this transcendental robe in which the German Socialists wrapped their sorry "eternal truths", all skin and bone, served to wonderfully increase the sale of their goods amongst such a public.

And on its part German Socialism recognised, more and more, its own calling as the bombastic representative of the petty-bourgeois Philistine.

It proclaimed the German nation to be the model nation, and the German petty Philistine to be the typical man. To every villainous meanness of this model man, it gave a hidden, higher, Socialistic interpretation, the exact contrary of its real character. It went to the extreme length of directly opposing the "brutally destructive" tendency of Communism, and of proclaiming its supreme and impartial contempt of all class struggles. With very few exceptions, all the so-called Socialist and Communist publications that now (1847) circulate in Germany belong to the domain of this foul and enervating literature.[‡]

[‡] The revolutionary storm of 1848 swept away this whole shabby tendency and cured its protagonists of the desire to dabble in socialism. The chief representative and classical type of this tendency is Mr Karl Gruen.

2. Conservative or Bourgeois Socialism

A part of the bourgeoisie is desirous of redressing social grievances in order to secure the continued existence of bourgeois society.

To this section belong economists, philanthropists, humanitarians, improvers of the condition of the working class, organisers of charity, members of societies for the prevention of cruelty to animals, temperance fanatics, hole-and-corner reformers of every imaginable kind. This form of socialism has, moreover, been worked out into complete systems.

We may cite Proudhon's *Philosophie de la Misère* as an example of this form.

The Socialistic bourgeois want all the advantages of modern social conditions without the struggles and dangers necessarily resulting therefrom. They desire the existing state of society, minus its revolutionary and disintegrating elements. They wish for a bourgeoisie without a proletariat. The bourgeoisie naturally conceives the world in which it is supreme to be the best; and bourgeois Socialism develops this comfortable conception into various more or less complete systems. In requiring the proletariat to carry out such a system, and thereby to march straightway into the social New Jerusalem, it but requires in reality, that the proletariat should remain within the bounds of existing society, but should cast away all its hateful ideas concerning the bourgeoisie.

A second, and more practical, but less systematic, form of this Socialism sought to depreciate every revolutionary movement in the eyes of the working class by showing that no mere political reform, but only a change in the material conditions of existence, in economical relations, could be of any advantage to them. By changes in the material conditions of existence, this form of Socialism, however, by no means understands abolition of the bourgeois relations of production, an abolition that can be affected only by a revolution, but administrative reforms, based on the continued existence of these relations; reforms, therefore, that in no respect affect the relations between capital and labour, but, at the best, lessen the cost, and simplify the administrative work, of bourgeois government.

Bourgeois Socialism attains adequate expression when, and only when, it becomes a mere figure of speech.

Free trade: for the benefit of the working class. Protective duties: for the benefit of the working class. Prison Reform: for the benefit of the working class. This is the last word and the only seriously meant word of bourgeois socialism.

Chapter III

It is summed up in the phrase: the bourgeois is a bourgeois – for the benefit of the working class.

3. Critical-Utopian Socialism and Communism

We do not here refer to that literature which, in every great modern revolution, has always given voice to the demands of the proletariat, such as the writings of Babeuf and others.

The first direct attempts of the proletariat to attain its own ends, made in times of universal excitement, when feudal society was being overthrown, necessarily failed, owing to the then undeveloped state of the proletariat, as well as to the absence of the economic conditions for its emancipation, conditions that had yet to be produced, and could be produced by the impending bourgeois epoch alone. The revolutionary literature that accompanied these first movements of the proletariat had necessarily a reactionary character. It inculcated universal asceticism and social levelling in its crudest form.

The Socialist and Communist systems, properly so called, those of Saint-Simon, Fourier, Owen, and others, spring into existence in the early undeveloped period, described above, of the struggle between proletariat and bourgeoisie (see Section I. Bourgeois and Proletarians).

The founders of these systems see, indeed, the class antagonisms, as well as the action of the decomposing elements in the prevailing form of society. But the proletariat, as yet in its infancy, offers to them the spectacle of a class without any historical initiative or any independent political movement.

Since the development of class antagonism keeps even pace with the development of industry, the economic situation, as they find it, does not as yet offer to them the material conditions for the emancipation of the proletariat. They therefore search after a new social science, after new social laws, that are to create these conditions.

Historical action is to yield to their personal inventive action; historically created conditions of emancipation to fantastic ones; and the gradual, spontaneous class organisation of the proletariat to an organisation of society especially contrived by these inventors. Future history resolves itself, in their eyes, into the propaganda and the practical carrying out of their social plans.

In the formation of their plans, they are conscious of caring chiefly for the interests of the working class, as being the most suffering class. Only from the point of view of being the most suffering class does the proletariat exist for them.

CHAPTER III

The undeveloped state of the class struggle, as well as their own surroundings, causes Socialists of this kind to consider themselves far superior to all class antagonisms. They want to improve the condition of every member of society, even that of the most favoured. Hence, they habitually appeal to society at large, without the distinction of class; nay, by preference, to the ruling class. For how can people, when once they understand their system, fail to see in it the best possible plan of the best possible state of society?

Hence, they reject all political, and especially all revolutionary action; they wish to attain their ends by peaceful means, necessarily doomed to failure, and by the force of example, to pave the way for the new social Gospel.

Such fantastic pictures of future society, painted at a time when the proletariat is still in a very undeveloped state and has but a fantastic conception of its own position, correspond with the first instinctive yearnings of that class for a general reconstruction of society.

But these Socialist and Communist publications contain also a critical element. They attack every principle of existing society. Hence, they are full of the most valuable materials for the enlightenment of the working class. The practical measures proposed in them – such as the abolition of the distinction be-tween town and country, of the family, of the carrying on of industries for the account of private individuals, and of the wage system, the proclamation of social harmony, the conversion of the function of the state into a more superintendence of production – all these proposals point solely to the disappearance of class antagonisms which were, at that time, only just cropping up, and which, in these publications, are recognised in their earliest indistinct and undefined forms only. These proposals, therefore, are of a purely Utopian character.

The significance of Critical-Utopian Socialism and Communism bears an inverse relation to historical development. In proportion as the modern class struggle develops and takes definite shape, this fan-tastic standing apart from the contest, these fantastic attacks on it, lose all practical value and all theoretical justification. Therefore, although the originators of these systems were, in many respects, revolutionary, their disciples have, in every case, formed mere reactionary sects. They hold fast by the original views of their masters, in opposition to the progressive historical development of the proletariat. They, there-fore, endeavour, and that consistently, to deaden the class struggle and to reconcile the class antagonisms.

CHAPTER III

They still dream of experimental realisation of their social Utopias, of founding isolated "phalansteres", of establishing "Home Colonies", or setting up a "Little Icaria"[§] – duodecimo editions of the New Jerusalem – and to realise all these castles in the air, they are compelled to appeal to the feelings and purses of the bourgeois. By degrees, they sink into the category of the reactionary [or] conservative Socialists depicted above, differing from these only by more systematic pedantry, and by their fanatical and superstitious belief in the miraculous effects of their social science.

They, therefore, violently oppose all political action on the part of the working class; such action, according to them, can only result from blind unbelief in the new Gospel.

[§] *Phalanstéres* were Socialist colonies on the plan of Charles Fourier; *Icaria* was the name given by Cabet to his Utopia and, later on, to his American Communist colony. "Home Colonies" were what Owen called his Communist model societies. *Phalanstéres* was the name of the public palaces planned by Fourier. *Icaria* was the name given to the Utopian land of fancy, whose Communist institutions Cabet portrayed.

The Owenites in England, and the Fourierists in France, respectively, oppose the Chartists and the *Réformistes*.

POSITION OF THE COMMUNISTS IN RELATION TO THE VARIOUS EXISTING OPPOSITION PARTIES

Section II has made clear the relations of the Communists to the existing working-class parties, such as the Chartists in England and the Agrarian Reformers in America.

The Communists fight for the attainment of the immediate aims, for the enforcement of the momentary interests of the working class; but in the movement of the present, they also represent and take care of the future of that movement. In France, the Communists ally with the Social-Democrats* against the conservative and radical bourgeoisie, reserving, however, the right to take up a critical position in regard to phases and illusions traditionally handed down from the great Revolution.

In Switzerland, they support the Radicals, without losing sight of the fact that this party consists of antagonistic elements, partly of Democratic Socialists, in the French sense, partly of radical bourgeois.

In Poland, they support the party that insists on an agrarian revolution as the prime condition for national emancipation, that party which fomented the insurrection of Cracow in 1846.

---

*The party then represented in Parliament by Ledru-Rollin, in literature by Louis Blanc, in the daily press by the *Réforme*. The name of Social-Democracy signifies, with these its inventors, a section of the Democratic or Republican Party more or less tinged with socialism.

In Germany, they fight with the bourgeoisie whenever it acts in a revolutionary way, against the absolute monarchy, the feudal squirearchy, and the petty bourgeoisie.

But they never cease, for a single instant, to instil into the working class the clearest possible recognition of the hostile antagonism between bourgeoisie and proletariat, in order that the German workers may straightway use, as so many weapons against the bourgeoisie, the social and political conditions that the bourgeoisie must necessarily introduce along with its supremacy, and in order that, after the fall of the reactionary classes in Germany, the fight against the bourgeoisie itself may immediately begin.

The Communists turn their attention chiefly to Germany, because that country is on the eve of a bourgeois revolution that is bound to be carried out under more advanced conditions of European civilisation and with a much more developed proletariat than that of England was in the seventeenth, and France in the eighteenth century, and because the bourgeois revolution in Germany will be but the prelude to an immediately following proletarian revolution.

In short, the Communists everywhere support every revolutionary movement against the existing social and political order of things.

CHAPTER IV

In all these movements, they bring to the front, as the leading question in each, the property question, no matter what its degree of development at the time.

Finally, they labour everywhere for the union and agreement of the democratic parties of all countries.

The Communists disdain to conceal their views and aims. They openly declare that their ends can be attained only by the forcible overthrow of all existing social conditions. Let the ruling classes tremble at a Communistic revolution. The proletarians have nothing to lose but their chains. They have a world to win.

Working Men of All Countries, Unite!

APPENDICES

LETTER FROM ENGELS TO MARX, 24 NOVEMBER 1847

Paris, 23-24 November 1847

Dear Marx,

Not until this evening was it decided that I should be coming. Saturday evening, then, in Ostend, Hôtel de la Couronne, just opposite the railway station beside the harbour, and Sunday morning across the water. If you take the train that leaves between 4 and 5, you'll arrive at about the same time as I do. ...

Tuesday evening

Verte [PTO]

Give a little thought to the "Confession of Faith." I think we would do best to abandon the catechetical form and call the thing "Communist Manifesto." Since a certain amount of history has to be narrated in it, the form hitherto adopted is quite unsuitable. I shall be bringing with me the one from here, which I did ["Principles of Communism"]; it is in simple narrative form, but wretchedly worded, in a tearing hurry. I start off by asking: What is communism? and then straight on to the proletariat – the history of its origins, how it differs from earlier workers, development of the antithesis between the proletariat and the bourgeoisie, crises, conclusions. In between, all kinds of secondary matter and, finally, the communists' party policy, in so far as it should be made public. The one here has not yet been submitted in its entirety for endorsement but, save for a few quite minor points, I think I can get it through in such a form that at least there is nothing in it which conflicts with our views. ...

DRAFT OF A COMMUNIST CONFESSION OF FAITH*

APPENDIX B

Question 1: *Are you a Communist?*
Answer: Yes.

Question 2: *What is the aim of the Communists?*
Answer: To organise society in such a way that every member of it can develop and use all his capabilities and powers in complete freedom and without thereby infringing the basic conditions of this society.

Question 3: *How do you wish to achieve this aim?*
Answer: By the elimination of private property and its replacement by community of property.

Question 4: *On what do you base your community of property?*
Answer: Firstly, on the mass of productive forces and means of subsistence resulting from the development of industry, agriculture, trade and colonisation, and on the possibility inherent in machinery, chemical and other resources of their infinite extension.

Secondly, on the fact that in the consciousness or feeling of every individual there exist certain irrefutable basic principles which, being the result of the whole of historical development, require no proof.

Question 5: *What are such principles?*

Answer: For example, every individual strives to be happy. The happiness of the individual is inseparable from the happiness of all, etc.

Question 6: *How do you wish to prepare the way for your community of property?*

Answer: By enlightening and uniting the proletariat.

Question 7: *What is the proletariat?*

Answer: The proletariat is that class of society which lives exclusively by its labour and not on the profit from any kind of capital; that class whose weal and woe, whose life and death, therefore, depend on the alternation of times of good and bad business;. in a word, on the fluctuations of competition.

Question 8: *Then there have not always been proletarians?*

Answer: No. There have always been *poor* and *working classes;* and those who worked were almost always the poor. But there have not always been proletarians, just as competition has not always been free.

Question 9: *How did the proletariat arise?*

Answer: The proletariat came into being as a result of the introduction of the machines which have been invented since the middle of the last century and the most important of which are: the steam-engine, the spinning machine and the power loom. These machines, which were very expensive and could therefore only be purchased by rich people, supplanted the workers of the time, because by the use of machinery it was possible to produce commodities more quickly and cheaply than could the workers with their imperfect spinning wheels and hand-looms. The machines thus delivered industry entirely into the hands of the big capitalists and rendered the workers' scanty property which consisted mainly of their tools, looms, etc., quite worthless, so that the capitalist was left with everything, the worker with nothing. In this way the factory system was introduced. Once the capitalists saw how advantageous this was for them, they sought to extend it to more and more branches of labour. They divided work more and more between the workers so that workers who formerly had made a whole article now produced only a part of it. Labour simplified in this way produced goods more quickly and therefore more cheaply and only now was it found in almost every branch of labour that here also machines could be used. As soon as any branch of labour went over to factory production it ended up, just as in the case of spinning and weaving, in the hands of the big capitalists, and the workers were deprived of the last remnants of their independence. We have gradually arrived at the position where almost *all* branches of labour are run on a factory basis. This has increasingly brought about the ruin of the previously existing middle class, especially of the small master craftsmen, completely transformed the previous position of the workers, and two new classes which are gradually swallowing up all other classes have come into being, namely:

I. The class of the big capitalists, who in all advanced countries are in almost exclusive possession of the means of subsistence and those means (machines, factories, workshops, etc.) by which these means of subsistence are produced. This is the *bourgeois* class, or the *bourgeoisie.*

II. The class of the completely propertyless, who are compelled to sell their labour to the first class, the bourgeois, simply to obtain from them in return their means of subsistence. Since the parties to this trading in labour are not *equal,* but the bourgeois have the advantage, the propertyless must submit to the bad conditions laid down by the bourgeois. This class, dependent on the bourgeois, is called the class of the *proletarians* or the *proletariat.*

Question 10: *In what way does the proletarian differ from the slave?*

Answer: The slave is sold once and for all, the proletarian has to sell himself by the day and by the hour.

The slave is the property of one master and for that very reason has a guaranteed subsistence, however wretched it may be. The proletarian is, so to speak, the slave of the entire bourgeois *class*, not of one master, and therefore has no guaranteed subsistence, since nobody buys his labour if he does not need it. The slave is accounted a *thing* and not a member of civil society. The proletarian is recognised as a *person*, as a member of civil society. The slave *may*, therefore, have a better subsistence than the proletarian but the latter stands at a higher stage of development. The slave frees himself by *becoming a proletarian*, abolishing from the totality of property relationships only the relationship of *slavery*. The proletarian can free himself only by abolishing *property in general*.

Question 11: *In what way does the proletarian differ from the serf?*

Answer: The serf has the use of a piece of land, that is, of an instrument of production, in return for handing over a greater or lesser portion of the yield. The proletarian works with instruments of production which belong to someone else who, in return for his labour, hands over to him a portion, determined by competition, of the products. In the case of the serf, the share of the labourer is determined by his own labour, that is, by himself. In the case of the proletarian it is determined by competition, therefore in the first place by the bourgeois. The serf has guaranteed subsistence, the proletarian has not. The serf frees himself by driving out his feudal lord and becoming a property owner himself, thus entering into competition and joining for the time being the possessing class, the privileged class. The proletarian frees himself by doing away with property, competition, and all class differences.

Question 12: *In what way does the proletarian differ from the handicraftsman?*

Answer: As opposed to the proletarian, the so-called handicraftsman, who still existed nearly everywhere during the last century and still exists here and there, is at most a temporary proletarian. His aim is to acquire capital himself and so to exploit other workers. He can often achieve this aim where the craft guilds still exist or where freedom to follow a trade has not yet led to the organisation of handwork on a factory basis and to intense competition. But as soon as the factory system is introduced into handwork and competition is in full swing, this prospect is eliminated and the handicraftsman becomes more and more a proletarian. The handicraftsman therefore frees himself *either* by becoming a bourgeois *or* in general passing over into the middle class, or, by becoming a proletarian as a result of competition (as now happens in most cases) and joining the movement of the proletariat – i.e., the more or less conscious communist movement.

Question 13: *Then you do not believe that community of property has been possible at any time?*

Answer: No. Communism has only arisen since machinery and other inventions made it possible to hold out the prospect of an all-sided development, a happy existence, for all members of society. Communism is the theory of a liberation which was not possible for the slaves, the serfs, or the handicraftsmen, but only for the proletarians and hence it belongs of necessity to the 19th century and was not possible in any earlier period.

Question 14: *Let me go back to the sixth question. As you wish to prepare for community of property by the enlightening and uniting of the proletariat, then you reject revolution?*

Answer: We are convinced not only of the uselessness but even of the harmfulness of all conspiracies. We are also aware that revolutions are not made deliberately and arbitrarily but that everywhere and at all times they are the necessary consequence of circumstances which are not in any way whatever dependent either on the will or on the leadership of individual parties or of whole classes. But we also see that the development of the proletariat in almost all countries of the world is forcibly repressed by the possessing classes and that thus a revolution is being forcibly worked for by the opponents of communism. If, in the end, the oppressed proletariat is thus driven into a revolution, then we will defend the cause of the proletariat just as well by our deeds as now by our words.

Question 15: *Do you intend to replace the existing social order by community of Property at one stroke?*

Answer: We have no such intention. The development of the masses cannot he ordered by decree. It is determined by the development of the conditions in which these masses live, and therefore proceeds gradually.

Question 16: *How do you think the transition from the present situation to community of Property is to be effected?*

Answer: The first, fundamental condition for the introduction of community of property is the political liberation of the proletariat through a democratic constitution.

Question 17: *What will be your first measure once you have established democracy?*

Answer: Guaranteeing the subsistence of the proletariat.

Question 18: *How will you do this?*

Answer. I: By limiting private property in such a way that it gradually prepares the way for its transformation into social property, e. g., by progressive taxation, limitation of the right of inheritance in favour of the state, etc., etc.

II. By employing workers in national workshops and factories and on national estates.

III. By educating all children at the expense of the state.

Question 19: *How will you arrange this kind of education during the period of transition?*

Answer: All children will be educated in state establishments from the time when they can do without the first maternal care.

Question 20: *Will not the introduction of community of property be accompanied by the proclamation of the* community of women?

Answer: By no means. We will only interfere in the personal relationship between men and women or with the family in general to the extent that the maintenance of the existing institution would disturb the new social order. Besides, we are well aware that the family relationship has been modified in the course of history by the property relationships and by periods of development, and that consequently the ending of private property will also have a most important influence on it.

Question 21: *Will nationalities continue to exist under communism?*

Answer: The nationalities of the peoples who join together according to the principle of community will be just as much compelled by this union to merge with one another and thereby supersede themselves as the various differences between estates and classes disappear through the superseding of their basis – private property.

Question 22. *Do Communists reject existing religions?*

Answer: All religions which have existed hitherto were expressions of historical stages of development of individual peoples or groups of peoples. But communism is that stage of historical development which makes all existing religions superfluous and supersedes them.

In the name and on the mandate of the Congress.

London, June 9, 1847

APPENDIX C

THE PRINCIPLES OF*
COMMUNISM

---

*Composed by Engels, October–November 1847.

Appendix C

1. What is Communism?

Communism is the doctrine of the conditions of the liberation of the proletariat.

2. What is the proletariat?

The proletariat is that class in society which lives entirely from the sale of its labour and does not draw profit from any kind of capital; whose weal and woe, whose life and death, whose sole existence depends on the demand for labour – hence, on the changing state of business, on the vagaries of unbridled competition. The proletariat, or the class of proletarians, is, in a word, the working class of the 19th century.

3. Proletarians, then, have not always existed?

No. There have always been poor and working classes; and the working class have mostly been poor. But there have not always been workers and poor people living under conditions as they are today; in other words, there have not always been proletarians, any more than there has always been free unbridled competitions.

4. How did the proletariat originate?

The Proletariat originated in the industrial revolution, which took place in England in the last half of the last (18th) century, and which has since then been repeated in all the civilized countries of the world.

This industrial revolution was precipitated by the discovery of the steam engine, various spinning machines, the mechanical loom, and a whole series of other mechanical devices. These machines, which were very expensive and hence could be bought only by big capitalists, altered the whole mode of production and displaced the former workers, because the machines turned out cheaper and better commodities than the workers could produce with their inefficient spinning wheels and handlooms. The machines delivered industry wholly into the hands of the big capitalists and rendered entirely worthless the meagre property of the workers (tools, looms, etc.). The result was that the capitalists soon had everything in their hands and nothing remained to the workers. This marked the introduction of the factory system into the textile industry.

Once the impulse to the introduction of machinery and the factory system had been given, this system spread quickly to all other branches of industry, especially cloth- and book-printing, pottery, and the metal industries.

Labour was more and more divided among the individual workers so that the worker who previously had done a complete piece of work now did only a part of that piece. This division of labour made it possible to produce things faster and cheaper. It reduced the activity of the individual worker to simple, endlessly repeated mechanical motions which could be performed not only as well but much better by a machine. In this way, all these industries fell, one after another, under the dominance of steam, machinery, and the factory system, just as spinning and weaving had already done.

But at the same time, they also fell into the hands of big capitalists, and their workers were deprived of whatever independence remained to them. Gradually, not only genuine manufacture but also handicrafts came within the province of the factory system as big capitalists increasingly displaced the small master craftsmen by setting up huge workshops, which saved many expenses and permitted an elaborate division of labour.

This is how it has come about that in civilized countries at the present time nearly all kinds of labour are performed in factories – and, in nearly all branches of work, handicrafts and manufacture have been superseded. This process has, to an ever greater degree, ruined the old middle class, especially the small handicraftsmen; it has entirely transformed the condition of the workers; and two new classes have been created which are gradually swallowing up all the others.

These are:

   i. The class of big capitalists, who, in all civilized countries, are already in almost exclusive possession of all the means of subsistence and of the instruments (machines, factories) and materials necessary for the production of the means of subsistence. This is the bourgeois class, or the bourgeoisie.

  ii. The class of the wholly propertyless, who are obliged to sell their labour to the bourgeoisie in order to get, in exchange, the means of subsistence for their support. This is called the class of proletarians, or the proletariat.

5. Under what conditions does this sale of the labour of the proletarians to the bourgeoisie take place?

Labour is a commodity, like any other, and its price is therefore determined by exactly the same laws that apply to other commodities. In a regime of big industry or of free competition – as we shall see, the two come to the same thing – the price of a commodity is, on the average, always equal to its cost of production. Hence, the price of labour is also equal to the cost of production of labour.

But, the costs of production of labour consist of precisely the quantity of means of subsistence necessary to enable the worker to continue working, and to prevent the working class from dying out. The worker will therefore get no more for his labour than is necessary for this purpose; the price of labour, or the wage, will, in other words, be the lowest, the minimum, required for the maintenance of life.

However, since business is sometimes better and sometimes worse, it follows that the worker sometimes gets more and sometimes gets less for his commodities. But, again, just as the industrialist, on the average of good times and bad, gets no more and no less for his commodities than what they cost, similarly on the average the worker gets no more and no less than his minimum.

This economic law of wages operates the more strictly the greater the degree to which big industry has taken possession of all branches of production.

6. What working classes were there before the industrial revolution?

The working classes have always, according to the different stages of development of society, lived in different circumstances and had different relations to the owning and ruling classes.

In antiquity, the workers were the slaves of the owners, just as they still are in many backward countries and even in the southern part of the United States.

In the Middle Ages, they were the serfs of the land-owning nobility, as they still are in Hungary, Poland, and Russia. In the Middle Ages, and indeed right up to the industrial revolution, there were also journeymen in the cities who worked in the service of petty bourgeois masters. Gradually, as manufacture developed, these journeymen became manufacturing workers who were even then employed by larger capitalists.

7. In what way do proletarians differ from slaves?

The slave is sold once and for all; the proletarian must sell himself daily and hourly.

The individual slave, property of one master, is assured an existence, however miserable it may be, because of the master's interest. The individual proletarian, property as it were of the entire bourgeois class which buys his labour only when someone has need of it, has no secure existence. This existence is assured only to the class as a whole.

The slave is outside competition; the proletarian is in it and experiences all its vagaries.

The slave counts as a thing, not as a member of society. Thus, the slave can have a better existence than the proletarian, while the proletarian belongs to a higher stage of social development and, himself, stands on a higher social level than the slave.

The slave frees himself when, of all the relations of private property, he abolishes only the relation of slavery and thereby becomes a proletarian; the proletarian can free himself only by abolishing private property in general.

8. In what way do proletarians differ from serfs?

The serf possesses and uses an instrument of production, a piece of land, in exchange for which he gives up a part of his product or part of the services of his labour.

The proletarian works with the instruments of production of another, for the account of this other, in exchange for a part of the product.

The serf gives up, the proletarian receives. The serf has an assured existence, the proletarian has not. The serf is outside competition, the proletarian is in it.

The serf liberates himself in one of three ways: either he runs away to the city and there becomes a handicraftsman; or, instead of products and services, he gives money to his lord and thereby becomes a free tenant; or he overthrows his feudal lord and himself becomes a property owner. In short, by one route or another, he gets into the owning class and enters into competition. The proletarian liberates himself by abolishing competition, private property, and all class differences.

9. In what way do proletarians differ from handicraftsmen?

In contrast to the proletarian, the so-called handicraftsman, as he still existed almost everywhere in the past (eighteenth) century and still exists here and there at present, is a proletarian at most temporarily. His goal is to acquire capital himself wherewith to exploit other workers. He can often achieve this goal where guilds still exist or where freedom from guild restrictions has not yet led to the introduction of factory-style methods into the crafts nor yet to fierce competition But as soon as the factory system has been introduced into the crafts and competition flourishes fully, this perspective dwindles away and the handicraftsman becomes more and more a proletarian. The handicraftsman therefore frees himself by becoming either bourgeois or entering the middle class in general, or becoming a proletarian because of competition (as is now more often the case). In which case he can free himself by joining the proletarian movement, i.e., the more or less communist movement.

10. In what way do proletarians differ from manufacturing workers?

The manufacturing worker of the 16th to the 18th centuries still had, with but few exception, an instrument of production in his own possession – his loom, the family spinning wheel, a little plot of land which he cultivated in his spare time. The proletarian has none of these things.

The manufacturing worker almost always lives in the countryside and in a more or less patriarchal relation to his landlord or employer; the proletarian lives, for the most part, in the city and his relation to his employer is purely a cash relation.

The manufacturing worker is torn out of his patriarchal relation by big industry, loses whatever property he still has, and in this way becomes a proletarian.

11. What were the immediate consequences of the industrial revolution and of the division of society into bourgeoisie and proletariat?

First, the lower and lower prices of industrial products brought about by machine labour totally destroyed, in all countries of the world, the old system of manufacture or industry based upon hand labour.

In this way, all semi-barbarian countries, which had hitherto been more or less strangers to historical development, and whose industry had been based on manufacture, were violently forced out of their isolation. They bought the cheaper commodities of the English and allowed their own manufacturing workers to be ruined. Countries which had known no progress for thousands of years – for example, India – were thoroughly revolutionized, and even China is now on the way to a revolution.

We have come to the point where a new machine invented in England deprives millions of Chinese workers of their livelihood within a year's time.

In this way, big industry has brought all the people of the Earth into contact with each other, has merged all local markets into one world market, has spread civilization and progress everywhere and has thus ensured that whatever happens in civilized countries will have repercussions in all other countries.

It follows that if the workers in England or France now liberate themselves, this must set off revolution in all other countries – revolutions which, sooner or later, must accomplish the liberation of their respective working class.

Second, wherever big industries displaced manufacture, the bourgeoisie developed in wealth and power to the utmost and made itself the first class of the country. The result was that wherever this happened, the bourgeoisie took political power into its own hands and displaced the hitherto ruling classes, the aristocracy, the guildmasters, and their representative, the absolute monarchy.

The bourgeoisie annihilated the power of the aristocracy, the nobility, by abolishing the entailment of estates – in other words, by making landed property subject to purchase and sale, and by doing away with the special privileges of the nobility. It destroyed the power of the guildmasters by abolishing guilds and handicraft privileges. In their place, it put competition – that is, a state of society in which everyone has the right to enter into any branch of industry, the only obstacle being a lack of the necessary capital.

The introduction of free competition is thus public declaration that from now on the members of society are unequal only to the extent that their capitals are unequal, that capital is the decisive power, and that therefore the capitalists, the bourgeoisie, have become the first class in society.

Free competition is necessary for the establishment of big industry, because it is the only condition of society in which big industry can make its way.

Having destroyed the social power of the nobility and the guildmasters, the bourgeois also destroyed their political power. Having raised itself to the actual position of first class in society, it proclaims itself to be also the dominant political class. This it does through the introduction of the representative system which rests on bourgeois equality before the law and the recognition of free competition, and in European countries takes the form of constitutional monarchy. In these constitutional monarchies, only those who possess a certain capital are voters – that is to say, only members of the bourgeoisie. These bourgeois voters choose the deputies, and these bourgeois deputies, by using their right to refuse to vote taxes, choose a bourgeois government.

Third, everywhere the proletariat develops in step with the bourgeoisie. In proportion, as the bourgeoisie grows in wealth, the proletariat grows in numbers. For, since the proletarians can be employed only by capital, and since capital extends only through employing labour, it follows that the growth of the proletariat proceeds at precisely the same pace as the growth of capital.

Simultaneously, this process draws members of the bourgeoisie and proletarians together into the great cities where industry can be carried on most profitably, and by thus throwing great masses in one spot it gives to the proletarians a consciousness of their own strength.

Moreover, the further this process advances, the more new labour-saving machines are invented, the greater is the pressure exercised by big industry on wages, which, as we have seen, sink to their minimum and therewith render the condition of the proletariat increasingly unbearable. The growing dissatisfaction of the proletariat thus joins with its rising power to prepare a proletarian social revolution.

12. What were the further consequences of the industrial revolution?

Big industry created in the steam engine, and other machines, the means of endlessly expanding industrial production, speeding it up, and cutting its costs. With production thus facilitated, the free competition, which is necessarily bound up with big industry, assumed the most extreme forms; a multitude of capitalists invaded industry, and, in a short while, more was produced than was needed.

As a consequence, finished commodities could not be sold, and a so-called commercial crisis broke out. Factories had to be closed, their owners went bankrupt, and the workers were without bread. Deepest misery reigned everywhere.

After a time, the superfluous products were sold, the factories began to operate again, wages rose, and gradually business got better than ever.

But it was not long before too many commodities were again produced and a new crisis broke out, only to follow the same course as its predecessor.

Ever since the beginning of this (19th) century, the condition of industry has constantly fluctuated between periods of prosperity and periods of crisis; nearly every five to seven years, a fresh crisis has intervened, always with the greatest hardship for workers, and always accompanied by general revolutionary stirrings and the direct peril to the whole existing order of things.

13. What follows from these periodic commercial crises?

First:

> That, though big industry in its earliest stage created free competition, it has now outgrown free competition;
>
> that, for big industry, competition and generally the individualistic organization of production have become a fetter which it must and will shatter;
>
> that, so long as big industry remains on its present footing, it can be maintained only at the cost of general chaos every seven years, each time threatening the whole of civilization and not only plunging the proletarians into misery but also ruining large sections of the bourgeoisie;
>
> hence, either that big industry must itself be given up, which is an absolute impossibility, or that it makes unavoidably necessary an entirely new organization of society in which production is no longer directed by mutually competing individual industrialists but rather by the whole society operating according to a definite plan and taking account of the needs of all.

Second: That big industry, and the limitless expansion of production which it makes possible, bring within the range of feasibility a social order in which so much is produced that every member of society will be in a position to exercise and develop all his powers and faculties in complete freedom.

It thus appears that the very qualities of big industry which, in our present-day society, produce misery and crises are those which, in a different form of society, will abolish this misery and these catastrophic depressions.

We see with the greatest clarity:

i. That all these evils are from now on to be ascribed solely to a social order which no longer corresponds to the requirements of the real situation; and

ii. That it is possible, through a new social order, to do away with these evils altogether.

14. What will this new social order have to be like?

Above all, it will have to take the control of industry and of all branches of production out of the hands of mutually competing individuals, and instead institute a system in which all these branches of production are operated by society as a whole – that is, for the common account, according to a common plan, and with the participation of all members of society.

It will, in other words, abolish competition and replace it with association.

Moreover, since the management of industry by individuals necessarily implies private property, and since competition is in reality merely the manner and form in which the control of industry by private property owners expresses itself, it follows that private property cannot be separated from competition and the individual management of industry. Private property must, therefore, be abolished and in its place must come the common utilization of all instruments of production and the distribution of all products according to common agreement – in a word, what is called the communal ownership of goods.

In fact, the abolition of private property is, doubtless, the shortest and most significant way to characterize the revolution in the whole social order which has been made necessary by the development of industry – and for this reason it is rightly advanced by communists as their main demand.

15. Was not the abolition of private property possible at an earlier time?

No. Every change in the social order, every revolution in property relations, is the necessary consequence of the creation of new forces of production which no longer fit into the old property relations.

Private property has not always existed.

When, towards the end of the Middle Ages, there arose a new mode of production which could not be carried on under the then existing feudal and guild forms of property, this manufacture, which had outgrown the old property relations, created a new property form, private property. And for manufacture and the earliest stage of development of big industry, private property was the only possible property form; the social order based on it was the only possible social order.

So long as it is not possible to produce so much that there is enough for all, with more left over for expanding the social capital and extending the forces of production – so long as this is not possible, there must always be a ruling class directing the use of society's productive forces, and a poor, oppressed class. How these classes are constituted depends on the stage of development.

The agrarian Middle Ages give us the baron and the serf; the cities of the later Middle Ages show us the guildmaster and the journeyman and the day labourer; the 17th century has its manufacturing workers; the 19th has big factory owners and proletarians.

It is clear that, up to now, the forces of production have never been developed to the point where enough could be developed for all, and that private property has become a fetter and a barrier in relation to the further development of the forces of production.

Now, however, the development of big industry has ushered in a new period. Capital and the forces of production have been expanded to an unprecedented extent, and the means are at hand to multiply them without limit in the near future. Moreover, the forces of production have been concentrated in the hands of a few bourgeois, while the great mass of the people are more and more falling into the proletariat, their situation becoming more wretched and intolerable in proportion to the increase of wealth of the bourgeoisie. And finally, these mighty and easily extended forces of production have so far outgrown private property and the bourgeoisie, that they threaten at any moment to unleash the most violent disturbances of the social order. Now, under these conditions, the abolition of private property has become not only possible but absolutely necessary.

16. Will the peaceful abolition of private property be possible?

It would be desirable if this could happen, and the communists would certainly be the last to oppose it. Communists know only too well that all conspiracies are not only useless, but even harmful. They know all too well that revolutions are not made intentionally and arbitrarily, but that, everywhere and always, they have been the necessary consequence of conditions which were wholly independent of the will and direction of individual parties and entire classes.

But they also see that the development of the proletariat in nearly all civilized countries has been violently suppressed, and that in this way the opponents of communism have been working toward a revolution with all their strength. If the oppressed proletariat is finally driven to revolution, then we communists will defend the interests of the proletarians with deeds as we now defend them with words.

17. Will it be possible for private property to be abolished at one stroke?

No, no more than existing forces of production can at one stroke be multiplied to the extent necessary for the creation of a communal society.

In all probability, the proletarian revolution will transform existing society gradually and will be able to abolish private property only when the means of production are available in sufficient quantity.

18. What will be the course of this revolution?

Above all, it will establish a democratic constitution, and through this, the direct or indirect dominance of the proletariat. Direct in England, where the proletarians are already a majority of the people. Indirect in

France and Germany, where the majority of the people consists not only of proletarians, but also of small peasants and petty bourgeois who are in the process of falling into the proletariat, who are more and more dependent in all their political interests on the proletariat, and who must, therefore, soon adapt to the demands of the proletariat. Perhaps this will cost a second struggle, but the outcome can only be the victory of the proletariat.

Democracy would be wholly valueless to the proletariat if it were not immediately used as a means for putting through measures directed against private property and ensuring the livelihood of the proletariat. The main measures, emerging as the necessary result of existing relations, are the following:

i. Limitation of private property through progressive taxation, heavy inheritance taxes, abolition of inheritance through collateral lines (brothers, nephews, etc.) forced loans, etc.

ii. Gradual expropriation of landowners, industrialists, railroad magnates and shipowners, partly through competition by state industry, partly directly through compensation in the form of bonds.

iii. Confiscation of the possessions of all emigrants and rebels against the majority of the people.

iv. Organization of labour or employment of proletarians on publicly owned land, in factories and workshops, with competition among the workers being abolished and with the factory owners, in so far as they still exist, being obliged to pay the same high wages as those paid by the state.

v. An equal obligation on all members of society to work until such time as private property has been completely abolished. Formation of industrial armies, especially for agriculture.

vi. Centralization of money and credit in the hands of the state through a national bank with state capital, and the suppression of all private banks and bankers.

vii. Increase in the number of national factories, workshops, railroads, ships; bringing new lands into cultivation and improvement of land already under cultivation – all in proportion to the growth of the capital and labour force at the disposal of the nation.

viii. Education of all children, from the moment they can leave their mother's care, in national establishments at national cost. Education and production together.

ix. Construction, on public lands, of great palaces as communal dwellings for associated groups of citizens engaged in both industry and agriculture and combining in their way of life the advantages of urban and rural conditions while avoiding the one-sidedness and drawbacks of each.

x. Destruction of all unhealthy and jerry-built dwellings in urban districts.

xi. Equal inheritance rights for children born in and out of wedlock.

xii. Concentration of all means of transportation in the hands of the nation.

It is impossible, of course, to carry out all these measures at once. But one will always bring others in its wake. Once the first radical attack on private property has been launched, the proletariat will find itself forced to go ever further, to concentrate increasingly in the hands of the state all capital, all agriculture, all transport, all trade. All the foregoing measures are directed to this end; and they will become practicable and feasible, capable of producing their centralizing effects to precisely the degree that the proletariat, through its labour, multiplies the country's productive forces.

Finally, when all capital, all production, all exchange have been brought together in the hands of the nation, private property will disappear of its own accord, money will become superfluous, and production will so expand and man so change that society will be able to slough off whatever of its old economic habits may remain.

19. Will it be possible for this revolution to take place in one country alone?

No. By creating the world market, big industry has already brought all the peoples of the Earth, and especially the civilized peoples, into such close relation with one another that none is independent of what happens to the others.

Further, it has co-ordinated the social development of the civilized countries to such an extent that, in all of them, bourgeoisie and proletariat have become the decisive classes, and the struggle between them the great struggle of the day. It follows that the communist revolution will not merely be a national phenomenon but must take place simultaneously in all civilized countries – that is to say, at least in England, America, France, and Germany.

It will develop in each of the these countries more or less rapidly, according as one country or the other has a more developed industry, greater wealth, a more significant mass of productive forces. Hence, it will go slowest and will meet most obstacles in Germany, most rapidly and with the fewest difficulties in England. It will have a powerful impact on the other countries of the world, and will radically alter the course of development which they have followed up to now, while greatly stepping up its pace.

It is a universal revolution and will, accordingly, have a universal range.

20. What will be the consequences of the ultimate disappearance of private property?

Society will take all forces of production and means of commerce, as well as the exchange and distribution of products, out of the hands of private capitalists and will manage them in accordance with a plan based on the availability of resources and the needs of the whole society. In this way, most important of all, the evil consequences which are now associated with the conduct of big industry will be abolished.

There will be no more crises; the expanded production, which for the present order of society is overproduction and hence a prevailing cause of misery, will then be insufficient and in need of being expanded much further. Instead of generating misery, overproduction will reach beyond the elementary requirements of society to assure the satisfaction of the needs of all; it will create new needs and, at the same time, the means of satisfying them. It will become the condition of, and the stimulus to, new progress, which will no longer throw the whole social order into confusion, as progress has always done in the past. Big industry, freed from the pressure of private property, will undergo such an expansion that what we now see will seem as petty in comparison as manufacture seems when put beside the big industry of our own day. This development of industry will make available to society a sufficient mass of products to satisfy the needs of everyone.

The same will be true of agriculture, which also suffers from the pressure of private property and is held back by the division of privately owned land into small parcels. Here, existing improvements and scientific procedures will be put into practice, with a resulting leap forward which will assure to society all the products it needs.

In this way, such an abundance of goods will be able to satisfy the needs of all its members.

The division of society into different, mutually hostile classes will then become unnecessary. Indeed, it will be not only unnecessary but intolerable in the new social order. The existence of classes originated in the division of labour, and the division of labour, as it has been known up to the present, will completely disappear. For mechanical and chemical processes are not enough to bring industrial and agricultural production up to the level we have described; the capacities of the men who make use of these processes must undergo a corresponding development.

Just as the peasants and manufacturing workers of the last century changed their whole way of life and became quite different people when they were drawn into big industry, in the same way, communal control over production by society as a whole, and the resulting new development, will both require an entirely different kind of human material.

People will no longer be, as they are today, subordinated to a single branch of production, bound to it, exploited by it; they will no longer develop *one* of their faculties at the expense of all others; they will no longer know only *one* branch, or one branch of a single branch, of production as a whole. Even industry as it is today is finding such people less and less useful.

Industry controlled by society as a whole, and operated according to a plan, presupposes well-rounded human beings, their faculties developed in balanced fashion, able to see the system of production in its entirety.

The form of the division of labour which makes one a peasant, another a cobbler, a third a factory worker, a fourth a stock-market operator, has already been undermined by machinery and will completely disappear. Education will enable young people quickly to familiarize themselves with the whole system of production and to pass from one branch of production to another in response to the needs of society or their own inclinations. It will, therefore, free them from the one-sided character which the present-day division of labour impresses upon every individual. Communist society will, in this way, make it possible for its members to put their comprehensively developed faculties to full use. But, when this happens, classes will necessarily disappear. It follows that society organized on a communist basis is incompatible with the existence of classes on the one hand, and that the very building of such a society provides the means of abolishing class differences on the other.

A corollary of this is that the difference between city and country is destined to disappear. The management of agriculture and industry by the same people rather than by two different classes of people is, if only for purely material reasons, a necessary condition of communist association. The dispersal of the agricultural population on the land, alongside the crowding of the industrial population into the great cities, is a condition which corresponds to an undeveloped state of both agriculture and industry and can already be felt as an obstacle to further development.

The general co-operation of all members of society for the purpose of planned exploitation of the forces of production, the expansion of production to the point where it will satisfy the needs of all, the abolition of a situation in which the needs of some are satisfied at the expense of the needs of others, the complete liquidation of classes and their conflicts, the rounded development of the capacities of all members of society through the elimination of the present division of labour, through industrial education, through engaging in varying activities, through the participation by all in the enjoyments produced by all, through the combination of city and country – these are the main consequences of the abolition of private property.

21. What will be the influence of communist society on the family?

It will transform the relations between the sexes into a purely private matter which concerns only the persons involved and into which society has no occasion to intervene. It can do this since it does away with private property and educates children on a communal basis, and in this way removes the two bases of traditional marriage – the dependence rooted in private property, of the women on the man, and of the children on the parents.

And here is the answer to the outcry of the highly moral philistines against the "community of women". Community of women is a condition which belongs entirely to bourgeois society and which today finds its complete expression in prostitution. But prostitution is based on private property and falls with it. Thus, communist society, instead of introducing community of women, in fact abolishes it.

22. What will be the attitude of communism to existing nationalities?

The nationalities of the peoples associating themselves in accordance with the principle of community will be compelled to mingle with each other as a result of this association and thereby to dissolve themselves, just as the various estate and class distinctions must disappear through the abolition of their basis, private property.

23. What will be its attitude to existing religions?

All religions so far have been the expression of historical stages of development of individual peoples or groups of peoples. But communism is the stage of historical development which makes all existing religions superfluous and brings about their disappearance.

24. How do communists differ from socialists?

The so-called socialists are divided into three categories.

[Reactionary Socialists:]

The first category consists of adherents of a feudal and patriarchal society which has already been destroyed, and is still daily being destroyed, by big industry and world trade and their creation, bourgeois society. This category concludes, from the evils of existing society, that feudal and patriarchal society must be restored because it was free of such evils. In one way or another, all their proposals are directed to this end.

This category of reactionary socialists, for all their seeming partisanship and their scalding tears for the misery of the proletariat, is nevertheless energetically opposed by the communists for the following reasons:

    i. It strives for something which is entirely impossible.

    ii. It seeks to establish the rule of the aristocracy, the guildmasters, the small producers, and their retinue of absolute or feudal monarchs, officials, soldiers, and priests – a society which was, to be sure, free of the evils of present-day society but which brought it at least as many evils without even offering to the oppressed workers the prospect of liberation through a communist revolution.

    iii. As soon as the proletariat becomes revolutionary and communist, these reactionary socialists show their true colours by immediately making common cause with the bourgeoisie against the proletarians.

[Bourgeois Socialists:]

The second category consists of adherents of present-day society who have been frightened for its future by the evils to which it necessarily gives rise. What they want, therefore, is to maintain this society while getting rid of the evils which are an inherent part of it.

To this end, some propose mere welfare measures – while others come forward with grandiose systems of reform which, under the pretence of re-organizing society, are in fact intended to preserve the foundations, and hence the life, of existing society.

Communists must unremittingly struggle against these bourgeois socialists because they work for the enemies of communists and protect the society which communists aim to overthrow.

[Democratic Socialists:]

Finally, the third category consists of democratic socialists who favour some of the same measures the communists advocate, as described in Question 18, not as part of the transition to communism, however, but as measures which they believe will be sufficient to abolish the misery and evils of present-day society.

These democratic socialists are either proletarians who are not yet sufficiently clear about the conditions of the liberation of their class, or they are representatives of the petty bourgeoisie, a class which, prior to the achievement of democracy and the socialist measures to which it gives rise, has many interests in common with the proletariat.

It follows that, in moments of action, the communists will have to come to an understanding with these democratic socialists, and in general to follow as far as possible a common policy with them – provided that these socialists do not enter into the service of the ruling bourgeoisie and attack the communists.

It is clear that this form of co-operation in action does not exclude the discussion of differences.

25. What is the attitude of the communists to the other political parties of our time?

This attitude is different in the different countries.

In England, France, and Belgium, where the bourgeoisie rules, the communists still have a common interest with the various democratic parties, an interest which is all the greater the more closely the socialistic measures they champion approach the aims of the communists – that is, the more clearly and definitely they represent the interests of the proletariat and the more they depend on the proletariat for support. In England, for example, the working-class Chartists[v] are infinitely closer to the communists than the democratic petty bourgeoisie or the so-called Radicals.

In America, where a democratic constitution has already been established, the communists must make the common cause with the party which will turn this constitution against the bourgeoisie and use it in the interests of the proletariat – that is, with the agrarian National Reformers.[vi]

In Switzerland, the Radicals, though a very mixed party, are the only group with which the communists can co-operate, and, among these Radicals, the Vaudois and Genevese are the most advanced.

In Germany, finally, the decisive struggle now on the order of the day is that between the bourgeoisie and the absolute monarchy. Since the communists cannot enter upon the decisive struggle between themselves and the bourgeoisie until the bourgeoisie is in power, it follows that it is in the interest of the communists to help the bourgeoisie to power as soon as possible in order the sooner to be able to overthrow it. Against the governments, therefore, the communists must continually support the radical liberal party, taking care to avoid the self-deceptions of the bourgeoisie and not fall for the enticing promises of benefits which a victory for the bourgeoisie would allegedly bring to the proletariat. The sole advantages which the proletariat would derive from a bourgeois victory would consist

i. in various concessions which would facilitate the unification of the proletariat into a closely knit, battle-worthy, and organized class; and

ii. in the certainly that, on the very day the absolute monarchies fall, the struggle between bourgeoisie and proletariat will start. From that day on, the policy of the communists will be the same as it now is in the countries where the bourgeoisie is already in power.